Finding Italian Roots

FINDING

Italian
Roots

The Complete Guide for Americans

by John Philip Colletta, Ph.D.

First published 1993
Updated and corrected 1996
Second printing 1997
Third printing 1998
Published by Genealogical Publishing Co., Inc.
1001 N. Calvert St., Baltimore, MD 21202
Library of Congress Catalogue Card Number 93-79083
International Standard Book Number 0-8063-1393-5
Made in the United States of America

Acknowledgments

The author wishes to thank Sallyann Amdur Sack, Sharon DeBartolo Carmack, Duilio and Corinne Puett Giannitrapani, Jayare Roberts and Robert Connelly for reading portions of this book in draft and offering helpful criticism and useful suggestions. The author also wishes to thank the staff members of the Family History Library of the Church of Jesus Christ of Latter-day Saints—Kory Meyerink, David Dilts, David Koldewyn, Diane Briggs and Terry Jeffs—for their assistance in securing illustrations for this volume. Cover design is by Robert Connelly; cover photograph is by Jim Vecchione.

For Grandma and Grandpa

Rosalia Girgenti (1892–1978)
Santo Colletta (1890–1964)

Contents

Americans Looking for Italian Records

In Italy there is little interest in genealogy. In the United States, however, Americans of Italian descent are tracing their roots in ever increasing numbers. Removed just two or three generations from their immigrant ancestors, most Italian Americans climbing their family tree reach the "Old Country" quickly and easily. The challenge they face then is to continue their family research in the records of their ancestors' homeland. More than ever, therefore, there is a demand for information about records in Italy. I have prepared this guide in response to that demand.

In three chapters I provide a detailed description of records of genealogical value in Italy. However, to help Americans find and use the Italian records most useful for their own family's story, I have included a substantial Introduction that explains the preparatory research they should perform in resources here in the United States; and in a Postscript I offer practical suggestions for getting the most out of the Italian records, whether in person or by mail. I conclude the guide with a Glossary of key Italian words and an extensive annotated Bibliography. In sum, I have tried to make this book a *complete* guide to Italian genealogy for Americans. (For an overview of works about Italian genealogy already in print, see the "Manuals for Italian Genealogy" section of the bibliography.)

Although the first Italian immigrant to the New World, Peter Caesar Alberti, came with the Dutch in 1635 and raised his family on Long Island, Italian immigration was extremely meager throughout the colonial period. (Historical facts throughout this book are derived from works cited in the bibliography and will not be individually footnoted.) The few Italians living in the United States by the early nineteenth century were mostly artisans, stonecutters, sculptors and painters from northern Italy. They tended to be political refugees or emigrants by choice. It was not until the 1870s and 1880s that Italians in significant numbers began to arrive. They settled for the most part in the rural, agricultural Deep South, as well as California, where the climate resembled that of their homeland. They opened "fancy fruits and vegetables" stands and restaurants; they planted vines brought from Italy and established wineries.

It was only after 1890 that economic necessity forced millions of Italians to seek work in America. The vast majority were peasants from the overpopulated, destitute southern regions of Italy, especially Calabria and Sicily, the so-called "Mezzogiorno." They were transplanted from sunny fishing villages on the Mediterranean coast and tiny farming communities in the interior mountains to the factories of America's northern industrial cities, the railroad construction sites in the Midwest and West, the iron mines of Minnesota and the copper and silver mines of Colorado. At first these laborers were called "birds of passage" because they came and went seasonally, working in the United States as long as weather permitted, then returning to their families in the Old Country for the winter months. Many remained birds of passage. But most who came once, twice, three times or more ended up bringing their wives and children and staying in America. (For more information about Italian immigration, see the "General Histories of Italians in America" section of the bibliography.)

Today the descendants of these Italian immigrants number in the millions and are spread throughout the United States. They participate in every facet of American life and culture, from cattle ranching in Montana to trawling for shrimp off the coast of Florida, from composing operas in Santa Fe to baking pasteries in Providence. In universities, corporations, city halls, sports arenas, theaters, state legislatures and governors' mansions across the country, in the U.S. Congress and the Supreme Court, there are descendants of Italian immigrants. And many of them are engaged in rediscovering their roots.

Introduction:
Preparation in
the United States

Whether you plan to conduct your genealogical research in Italian records by traveling to Italy or by corresponding with Italian repositories, it is essential that you prepare thoroughly by using the materials available in the United States first. Without adequate preparation you will not succeed in finding the Italian records that pertain to your family, or you may eventually find them after spending unnecessary time, effort and money. In addition, unless you leave your family research entirely in the hands of a professional genealogist, sooner or later you will have to acquire at least a minimal ability to read and write Italian. Otherwise, you will not be able to understand the informational content of your family's records once you locate them.

As your research progresses deeper and deeper into history, it will become necessary for you to decipher a variety of archaic handwritings, and probably to read some Latin, too. But these skills you may acquire and hone along the way. You start out with what is already familiar and accessible to you. Before describing the Italian records which will allow you to discover your family's story, therefore, it is appropriate to explain how you prepare to locate and utilize those records.

Three Basic Facts You Need to Know

First of all, you must know three basic facts about your immigrant ancestor:

Full Original Name. Many Italian surnames have been transformed in the United States—shortened, Americanized, spelled differently, changed completely. The reasons for this, and the family stories about surname changes, are myriad. Whatever the history of your own surname may be, to pursue your genealogical research in Italian records you must first learn what your immigrant ancestor's original surname was, and given name (or names) too.

Approximate Date of Birth. Given the Italian custom for naming children (see Postscript following chapter 3), many men and women in every extended family have identical names. Knowing your immigrant ancestor's birth date enables you to distinguish him from numerous cousins having the same name.

Town of Birth. Most civil and religious records in Italy are kept on the local level (see chapters 1 and 2). Genealogical research is impossible, therefore, without knowing the *comune* (town) where your immigrant ancestor was born. (Throughout this book, the first time an Italian term appears it is followed by its English translation in parentheses. Once introduced, however, the term will be used without translation, because the Italian terms are the ones you must know to use Italian records.)

Where You Find These Three Basic Facts

There are many ways you can discover the three basic facts about your immigrant ancestor. Rarely will you find all the facts in a single source. Rather, you will have to gather them or deduce them by combining information gleaned from a variety of sources.

Interviewing Relatives. Since most Americans of Italian descent are removed just two or three generations from their immigrant ancestors, interviewing relatives is especially productive. Older relatives who knew your immigrant ancestor, or the first generation of your family in America, are likely to have heard stories about the immigration experience: who came when, from where, and how and why. They may have heard anecdotes about the family's native village in Italy. Learn as much as you can about the town of your ancestors, for many towns in Italy have the same or similar name: what is the nearest major city, and how far is it from that city; how many churches are there in the village, and what are they called; is there a railroad station? . . . Such details may mean the difference between success and failure in distinguishing the town you want from others of the same name. Elderly relatives will often know the name of the steamship that brought your immigrant ancestor to America, and they may have been told stories about how the family's surname changed, and why. There is no way of knowing what fascinating and useful information your elderly relatives' memories may hold until you start asking questions.

Interviewing relatives not only gives you the fundamental facts on which all of your future research will be based, but provides personal information about your Italian ancestors as real people with individual personalities as well, and this information can often supply valuable clues as to what path your research should take in Italian records. Learning an ancestor's occupation, for example, might lead you to explore a resource you would not otherwise have ever thought of searching. Effective interviewing, however, is not magic. There are techniques to be employed and etiquette to be observed. Guidelines for conducting productive interviews are explained in books about recording oral history and in some genealogical manuals (see bibliography).

Using Materials at Home. Also because most Italian Americans are removed just two or three generations from their immigrant ancestors, exploiting family materials at home is especially effective for securing the basic facts about the immigrant ancestor. Passports, letters, photographs, military discharge papers, citizenship certificates, remembrance cards from funerals, steamship ticket stubs, postcards showing the town of origin, personal mementoes—these are all valuable sources of information (see illustrations on pp. 21–23). Many Italian families in the United States have at least one elderly relative—a spinster aunt, a great-uncle—who is known to have amassed such keepsakes over the years. Discover which family members might possess such documents in the course of your interviewing. Then contact those relatives and examine the family treasures while their location is still known.

Like interviewing, keepsakes found at home often reveal more about your ancestors than just the bare facts of their immigration story. Insight into an ancestor's temperament or motives may show up in the most unexpected places. An old tattered passbook, for instance, from the *Casse di Risparmio Postale* (Postal Savings Bank) of Rome, showing that your ancestor sent monthly deposits until late 1929, reveals that the immigrant intended to return to Italy one day, but the Depression intervened and ultimately caused him or her to remain in America. When examining family materials saved by a relative, therefore, be alert and overlook no clue to a better understanding of your Italian ancestors' stories.

Published Materials in Libraries. Published materials in libraries are increasingly important for Americans tracing Italian ancestors because works pertaining to Italian–American history have been multiplying rapidly over the past two decades. Before the American Bicentennial and the publication of *Roots*, before the popularity of ethnic cooking and the beginning of annual ethnic festivals in American cities, before scholars undertook their reexamination of immigration history and their reevaluation of the "melting pot" theory, genealogy in the United States was

Portion of passport belonging to Rosalia Girgenti and her son and daughter, Ignazio and Rosalia Colletta. Note that the mother appears under her maiden name, while the children are under their father's surname. Interior pages provide additional information about the family. (*From the author's collection.*)

First page of 4-page military discharge papers of Santo Colletta dated 1 February 1913. Interior pages contain a wealth of information about the soldier and his family. (*From the author's collection.*)

Steamship ticket stub showing receipt of payment for three 3rd class places on the SS *Patria*, leaving Palermo on 1 February 1920. Note that the mother is listed under her maiden name and pays full fare; child's place costs one-half fare, baby's place costs one-quarter. Reverse of stub informs passengers of meals to be provided on board and suggests additional provisions to bring. (*From the author's collection.*)

primarily the avocation of descendants of early English colonial settlers. Over the past twenty years, however, that has changed dramatically. Now Americans of all national heritages are engaged in tracing their roots, and this rise in ethnic interest and pride has engendered a boom in the publishing industry.

The bibliography at the end of this guide includes a selection of books and articles representative of the kinds of published resources useful to Americans researching Italian ancestors, which are now appearing in bookstores and libraries. Here, for example, are two types of works that can be useful for discovering the three basic facts about your immigrant ancestor:

Collective Biographies of Italian Americans. Collective biographies such as Carlevale's *Who's Who among Americans of Italian Descent in Connecticut* or the *Directory of Italian-Americans in Commerce and Professions* contain thousands of biographical sketches of Italian Americans living in the United States at the time of publication. You might find your immigrant ancestor discussed in such a work. If not, in the course of searching you might come across other, unfamiliar individuals with your family name. Noting where they came from in Italy may help localize the geographic area where your own people lived, and that knowledge will help establish the geographic parameters of your research in Italian records. In addition, taking note of surnames which differ from your own by only one or two letters may also be useful, since one or more of these may turn out to be historical "variants" of your own name. Throughout your research remain alert to all possible variant spellings of your surname, just to be sure you do not overlook any lead to further information.

Histories of Italian Communities in the United States. Detailed accounts of the historical development of Italian communities in specific cities, such as Schiavo's *The Italians in Chicago: A Study of Americanization*, and specific states, such as Starr's *The Italians of New Jersey: A Historical Introduction and Bibliography*, and specific geographic regions, such as Casso's *Staying in Step: A Continuing Italian Renaissance (A Saga of American-Italians in Southeast United States)*, are becoming ever more numerous. If you find such a history of the Italian community where your own family settled, it may contain the information you need about your immigrant ancestor. Even if your ancestor is not named, though, such works still provide valuable historical background against which you can better understand the facts of your ancestor's immigration story.

Collective biographies of Italian Americans and histories of Italian communities in the United States may only be found through conscientious searching in libraries with substantial collections. University libraries tend to be rich in these types of books, since many of them grow out of doctoral dissertations. Research centers that house Italian-American collections (see below) are also likely to have such books.

Federal Records. Federal records constitute a key source for learning the facts you need to know about your immigrant ancestor. Although these are discussed thoroughly in other genealogical manuals, a few words are offered here to illustrate how federal resources may be of particular value when searching for ancestors from Italy.

Censuses. The 1900, 1910 and 1920 censuses can be particularly helpful because they provide a date of immigration for residents born overseas, and indicate whether or not the resident has been naturalized (see illustration on p. 26). Earlier censuses do not contain this information, but most Italian immigrants were not yet in this country to be enumerated in those earlier censuses. If your ancestors were living in the United States by 1900, 1910 or 1920, therefore, the immigration and citizenship information in

Federal Census of 1910 for Haverstraw, Rockland County, New York, showing Geraci family on lines 51–62. Immigration and citizenship data are given in columns 15 and 16. Note that the immigrant who arrived in 1898, Joseph Geraci, is doing well enough in his bakery business by 1910 to employ four recent immigrants from Italy—a typical situation. (*Photograph courtesy of the Latter-day Saints Family History Library.*)

a federal census will help lead the way to ships' passenger lists, naturalization records, and continued research in Italy—unless your ancestors happened to be on a return trip to Italy the day the census enumerator came calling!

Federal censuses are available at the National Archives in Washington, D.C., the thirteen Regional Archives of the National Archives (see list on p. 28), and numerous libraries, including the Latter-day Saints Family History Library in Salt Lake City (cited hereafter as LDS FHL). The 1900 and 1920 censuses are fully indexed, 1900 by individual name, 1920 by household and unrelated individuals; but the 1910 census is only indexed for twenty-one states.

Ships' Passenger Lists. Perhaps the busiest port of arrival for Italian immigrants in the 1870s and 1880s was New Orleans. Some of the new arrivals stayed in the Crescent City. Others settled on farm land in rural Louisiana and Mississippi. Still others chose to continue up the Mississippi River and open markets for fresh fruits and vegetables in Baton Rouge, Natchez, Vicksburg, Memphis, Saint Louis and other cities where river commerce ensured brisk business. This settlement pattern explains the concentration of Italian Americans still residing in those areas today.

By the 1890s, though, the vast majority of Italian immigrants were arriving at the ports of New York, Boston, Philadelphia and Baltimore, where their numbers swelled to record highs in the early years of the twentieth century. Most of these were laborers with no particular skill or trade, so entrepreneurship was much more limited among them than it had been among the Italians who had arrived earlier in the South. These Italian laborers remained in the "Little Italys" of New York, Boston, Philadelphia and Baltimore. Or they moved on to employment opportunities in heavy industry and manufacturing in other cities of the North, such as Buffalo and Pittsburgh, where they also formed their own community.

National Archives—Regional Centers

National Archives and Records
Administration
8th Street and Pennsylvania
Avenue, NW
Washington, DC 20408

National Archives—New
England Region
380 Trapelo Road
Waltham, MA 02154
(serves CT, ME, MA, NH, RI and
VT)

National Archives—Pittsfield
Region
100 Dan Fox Drive
Pittsfield, MA 01201
(serves CT, ME, MA, NH, RI and
VT, microfilm only)

National Archives—Northeast
Region
201 Varick Street
New York, NY 10014
(serves NJ, NY, PR and VI)

National Archives—Mid-
Atlantic Region
9th and Market Streets,
Room 1350
Philadelphia, PA 19107
(serves DE, PA, MD, VA and WV)

National Archives—Great
Lakes Region
7358 South Pulaski Road
Chicago, IL 60629
(serves IL, IN, MI, MN, OH and WI)

National Archives—Southeast
Region
1557 Saint Joseph Avenue
East Point, GA 30344
(serves AL, GA, FL, KY, MS, NC,
SC and TN)

National Archives—Central
Plains Region
2312 East Bannister Road
Kansas City, MO 64131
(serves IO, KS, MO and NE)

National Archives—Southwest
Region
501 West Felix Street
PO Box 6216
Fort Worth, TX 76115
(serves AR, LA, NM, OK and TX)

National Archives—Rocky
Mountain Region
Building 48, Denver Federal
Center
Denver, CO 80225
(serves CO, MT, ND, SD, UT and
WY)

National Archives—Pacific
Sierra Region
1000 Commodore Drive
San Bruno, CA 94066
(serves northern CA, HI, NV
(except Clark County) and the
Pacific Ocean area)

National Archives—Pacific
Southwest Region
24000 Avila Road
PO Box 6719
Laguna Niguel, CA 92656
(serves AZ, the southern CA
counties of Imperial, Inyo, Kern,
Los Angeles, Orange, Riverside,
San Bernadino, San Diego, San
Luis Obispo, Santa Barbara and
Ventura, and Clark County, NV)

National Archives—Pacific
Northwest Region
6125 San Point Way, NE
Seattle, WA 98115
(serves ID, OR and WA)

National Archives—Alaska
Region
Federal Office Building
654 West Third Avenue,
Room 012
Anchorage, AK 99501
(serves Alaska)

Passenger list of the SS *Re d'Italia*, arriving in New York on 10 March 1910, showing the Anzelmo family on lines 17–20. Note the numerous notations and corrections made by the clerk at Ellis Island (including for Francesco Anzelmo—"Probate Court Geauga Co. Ohio Nov. 7, 1904") to clarify citizenship status of each member of an immigrant family returning to the United States after a sojourn in Italy. (*Photograph courtesy of the Latter-day Saints Family History Library.*)

By the turn of the century, Italians in considerable numbers were also arriving at New Bedford, Massachusetts, and settling in Rhode Island. In the South, the port of Galveston, Texas, received large numbers of Italians who settled throughout the Lone Star State. Ports on the Great Lakes, such as Duluth and Milwaukee, Detroit, Chicago and Cleveland, constituted the major point of arrival for Italians immigrating into the United States via Canada. Many of these laborers went to work in the mines of Minnesota's iron range; others ended up in the copper and silver mines of Colorado. And San Francisco remained the major Pacific Coast port of arrival for Italians headed for the vineyards of California and the cattle ranches of the Northwest.

For all of these ports and all of these years there are ships' passenger lists containing a variety of information about the Italians coming to America (see illustration on p. 29). While prior to 1906 these lists indicate only the "nationality" or "country of origin" or "last permanent residence" of each passenger on board, beginning in 1906 they provide the precise town of birth. If your Italian ancestor immigrated in 1906 or later, therefore, the ship's passenger list will be especially helpful in pursuing your family research, for it will give you the name of your ancestral *comune* in Italy.

Since passenger lists were prepared at the port of embarkation, your ancestor's name will appear as he or she pronounced it, or perhaps as it was written on your ancestor's passport. This surname may differ from the one you use today. Finding your ancestor's ship's passenger list, therefore, may turn out to be crucial to learning what surname you will be tracing in the records of Italy.

If an Italian ancestress was unmarried when she came to the United States, or was married but traveling without her husband, the ship's list will give you her maiden name. For that is the surname under which she appears in the list.

Women in Italy have always conducted official business of all kinds under their own family name, not their husband's, and this custom is reflected in the old ships' passenger lists. In the case where an Italian woman was coming to join her husband in the United States, and was bringing their children with her, she was listed under her maiden name, but the children were listed under their father's surname. When a married Italian woman was traveling with her husband, though, she was listed under her husband's surname.

For complete information about finding the passenger list of the ship that brought your ancestor to America, see *They Came in Ships: A Guide to Finding Your Immigrant Ancestor's Arrival Record*, cited in the bibliography.

Naturalization Records. It is possible that you may not find your immigrant ancestor's ship's passenger list because he or she appears in the list under a surname different from the one your family uses today. Never suspecting that at some time the surname underwent a transformation, you spend your time hunting for the wrong name. This dilemma may sometimes be remedied by using naturalization records. For in addition to the basic biographical facts about the immigrant provided in naturalization records, there is also information about his or her immigration, including sometimes the name of the ship and the port and date of arrival. Finding your ancestor's naturalization record, therefore, may direct you to the passenger list, which may alert you to a name change you never knew occurred.

Names of Italian immigrants appearing in naturalization records often differ from those in ships' passenger lists because the immigrant's first few years in America—the years between arriving and petitioning for citizenship—constitute the time period when a surname change most often occurred. Unfortunately, though, naturalization records do not always provide the name of the immigrant's ship or his port and date of arrival. More unfortunate still for Americans seeking Italian ancestors is the fact that relatively few Italian immigrants sought U.S. citizenship. Though many declared their intention to become citizens, very few petitioned for naturalization. The majority remained alien residents.

Naturalization records made in federal courts are available at the National Archives or one of its thirteen Regional Archives. Naturalizations made in state courts are found in county courthouses. And naturalizations made in municipal courts are generally preserved at city hall. Since September 27, 1906, a copy of all naturalization records made in all courts—federal, state and municipal—has been filed with the Immigration and Naturalization Service, 425 I Street NW, Washington, DC 20536, which maintains a master index, 1906–1956. In addition, numerous published indexes and finding aids for locating your immigrant ancestor's naturalization record can be found in libraries.

The National Archives has microfilmed card indexes to naturalizations filed in many courts around the country. These indexes are arranged by surname in alphabetical order and provide sufficient information about the naturalization to locate the original record. Most of them cover a single U.S. District Court; however, a few of them index naturalizations made in state and local courts. For example, one index of particular value for Italian Americans covers all naturalizations made in federal, state and local courts of New York City, 1792–1906.

Passport Applications. Prior to 1941, except for brief periods during wars, passports were not required for Americans to travel overseas or to re-enter the United States. Some Americans applied for and received a passport; others did not bother. Italians who became American citizens and then returned to Italy to visit relatives or bring back a wife and children frequently carried

U.S. passport application of Vincenzo Abbatticllo, dated 2 November 1904. Note that the complete facts of the alien's immigration and naturalization history are supplied. (*Photograph courtesy of the Latter-day Saints Family History Library.*)

only their certificate of naturalization with them for re-entry. Others proudly went through the process of obtaining a U.S. passport. Passport applications from 1791 through 1925 are available at the National Archives (see illustration on p. 33), and there are registers and indexes to help you search them. The passport applications and the registers and indexes are available on microfilm through the LDS FHL as well as the National Archives.

One of the advantages of locating a passport application for a naturalized citizen is that it contains the date and court of naturalization. It may also state the exact date and place of birth of the applicant, and of his wife and minor children, too. Applications since 1914 also contain the applicant's photograph, and his or her immediate travel plans, including the "reason for return" to Italy. Given the history of Italian immigration, therefore, and particularly the birds of passage phenomenon, it is easy to see why your immigrant ancestor's passport application would help you in preparing to do research in Italian records . . . if your ancestor applied for one.

Other Federal Records. Other federal records—such as World War I Draft Registration Cards, or records of immigrants entering the United States via Canada, which are available on microfilm at the National Archives and the LDS FHL—may also be useful in preparing to find and use Italian records. It all depends on the activities of your immigrant ancestor. Each one's story is unique. Different sources are helpful for different stories. Federal records, however, are not the only sources to turn to for the basic facts about your immigrant ancestor. Records kept on the state level may also prove useful.

State Censuses. Of all state-level records, state censuses may be singled out for special mention here as a particularly valuable resource for tracing Italian immigrants in the United States. They complement federal censuses as they were often enumerated in years between federal censuses. Especially noteworthy is that nearly all of the federal population schedules for 1890 were destroyed in a fire. But New York State, for example, conducted several censuses during the era when many Italian families were arriving and making the state their new home: 1892, 1905, 1915 and 1925. This was typical of many other states as well.

State censuses frequently indicate how long each resident has been living in the state, and the year when alien residents or naturalized citizens first arrived in the United States. Some New York State censuses even give the place of naturalization. Remember, many Italian birds of passage came to America once, twice or more before bringing their wives and children to join them. Then, once established in the United States, an Italian family might change residence several times before settling at one address. Combining information from state censuses with information from federal censuses, therefore, often establishes the chronology of an Italian family, showing when moves were made and which children were born where.

In addition, Italian families often played host to new immigrants for brief periods of time. A bird of passage might reside with a cousin, an in-law, an uncle, or a former neighbor from the *paese* (native countryside) for a year or two, or maybe for just a few months, until he was financially able to move into a place of his own and send for his family. When these brief stays did not happen to fall in years when federal censuses were enumerated, no federal record of them exists. But censuses taken on the state level in the "off years" may capture such a sojourn and provide essential information about your ancestor's immigration and citizenship status at the time.

Original state census schedules are generally kept in the state archives, library or historical society. Many have been microfilmed, however, and are easily accessible through the LDS FHL and local libraries.

If you find that records kept on the state level do not yield the three basic facts you need in order to pursue your family research in Italian records, local records are available for examination too.

Local Records. There are many local resources—described in detail in other genealogical manuals—that may possibly provide the essential facts you need to know about your immigrant ancestor. Here is a sampling of three local resources that are particularly useful for researching Italian families in America:

Cemetery Records. The record of your immigrant ancestor's burial may reveal the original spelling of his or her surname, date of birth, even the precise town of birth in Italy. Such records are usually found in the cemetery office, although older ones may have been removed to a local historical society, library or archives. Similar information may be included in the sexton's records in the city or county where your immigrant ancestor died.

Inscriptions on your ancestor's tombstone may include not only his or her name, but dates of birth and death, and native town as well. Furthermore, artwork on the tombstone is sometimes instructive: the decoration may contain symbols representing your ancestor's religion, occupation, fraternal affiliation in the United States, military involvement or place of origin. In Italy, traditional symbols identified the craft or trade of the deceased; these varied from one area of Italy to another. Italian-American sculptors sometimes carried these over into their work for Italian-American families here in the United States, thereby revealing more about a deceased person on his or her tombstone than would appear evident at first sight. Also quite common on the tombstones of late nineteenth- and early twentieth-century burials—at least in cemeteries in Texas and Louisiana—are photographs of the deceased. This, too, was a tradition brought to America by Italian immigrants (see "Italian Cemeteries" in the Postscript).

If your ancestor from Italy worked as a craftsman and belonged to the *società* (guild or society) for his craft, he may be buried in a "society vault." These mausoleums were built in cemeteries in some states, especially Louisiana— Lake Lawn Metairie Cemetery in New Orleans is the pre-eminent example (see illustrations on p. 38)—by the members of the *società* who pooled their savings to insure a decent burial for themselves and their families. Such vaults are generally surmounted by a statue of the patron saint of the craft, and decorated all around with sculpture and engravings representative of the trade. Members were often from the same town or village in Italy, and this is clearly reflected in the identity of the patron saint and the decoration.

Newspapers. An obituary for your immigrant ancestor, or a wedding or anniversary notice, may have appeared in his or her local newspaper, perhaps with a note to the local Italian language newspaper to "please copy." There were many newspapers printed in Italian in the late nineteenth and early twentieth century in the United States, and you are more likely to find information about your Italian ancestors in these than in the English language press. For the Italian papers focused on matters of interest and importance to the Italian community. New York City, for example, had at least ten newspapers in Italian, one of which, the *Eco d'Italia* (*Echo of Italy*), was published from 1849 through 1937. Chicago, Cincinnati, Buffalo, St. Louis, Boston, Philadelphia, Baltimore and numerous other smaller cities also had at least one or two Italian language newspapers each.

Most of these Italian language newspapers are no longer published, and there is no catalog or listing of them all. You

Italian society vaults in Lake Lawn Metairie Cemetery, New Orleans.
(*Photographs by the author.*)

must check the libraries of the state and community where your ancestors lived. Some newspapers in Italian are available on microfilm. *Newspapers in Microform: United States, 1948–1983,* 2 vols. (Washington, D.C.: Library of Congress, 1984) lists many nineteenth- and early twentieth-century Italian language newspapers that were microfilmed and reported to the Library of Congress by libraries across the country between 1948 and 1983. The Immigration History Research Center at the University of Minnesota in St. Paul is microfilming Italian language newspapers from around the country. For a list of those already filmed, see: *Report on the Italian American Newspaper Microfilming Project,* compiled by Timo Riippa in 1992. The great advantage of such microfilm is that it may be borrowed from the Center through the interlibrary loan system. For a list of Italian language newspapers still in print today, see Lubomyr R. and Anna T. Wynar's *Encyclopedic Directory of Ethnic Newspapers and Periodicals in the United States,* 2nd ed. (Littleton, Col.: Libraries Unlimited, Inc., 1976), pages 100–108.

Furthermore, the gossip columns of English language newspapers in rural areas sometimes noted the arrival of Italian immigrants in the community, or the appearance of Italian visitors. Society columns in urban newspapers often reported when Italian-American citizens known in the community—a restaurant owner, a grocer or baker, a businessman or lawyer—left for Italy to visit relatives, and when they returned home again.

Church Records. The sacramental registers of parishes in Italian neighborhoods of American cities can be especially valuable because the priests who created them retained something of the traditions of their native Italy. This means that the records of Italian parishes tend to contain more information about the people involved than do those of non-Italian parishes. For instance, the Confirmation record of an Italian parishioner, or his or her marriage record, often includes the name of the parish where the person was baptized, and sometimes the actual facts of the baptismal record as well. The relationship of sponsors or witnesses to the principals of the sacred event may also be stated, as it is in Italian church registers (see chapter 2).

Other Local Records. Other local records, such as city directories or city censuses (there is an 1892 Police Census of New York City by neighborhood), might also prove helpful in finding the key facts you must know about your immigrant ancestor before you can turn to Italian records. What you find depends on where your ancestors lived and how they participated in the work and social life of their community.

Additional Information You Can Gather

Before going to Italy or corresponding with Italian repositories, you can often discover much more about your immigrant ancestor than simply his or her full original name, approximate date of birth and town of birth. The more you know about your ancestor's family, the more productive and successful your work in Italian records will be. So you should conduct some additional research on your family here at home before traveling to Italy or beginning your correspondence.

Where You Find This Additional Information

Where do you perform this additional preparatory searching? — In the published, microfilmed and computerized Italian sources available in the United States. Here, for example, selected from the bibliography at the end of this guide, are five types of published works which are useful for securing additional information that will help you find and use the Italian records pertaining to your family:

Dictionaries of Italian Surnames. Works like
DeFelice's *Dizionario dei Cognomi Italiani* (*Dictionary of*

Italian Surnames) and Fucilla's *Our Italian Surnames* provide the possible origin and meaning of Italian family names. They indicate the particular geographic area or areas of Italy where each name, and its antecedents, derived and is concentrated. This information may help localize your research efforts if you have not yet discovered your ancestors' exact town. The etymology of your name also hints at where your family research may eventually lead you—Greece . . . Germany . . . Austria . . . France. . . . In addition, by noting those family names which vary only slightly from yours, you are gaining insight into the possible original spelling, or possible variant spellings, of your own name.

Italian National Biographies.
Works such as the *Dizionario Biografico degli Italiani* (*Biographical Dictionary of the Italians*) or the *Enciclopedia Biografica e Bibliografica Italiana* (*Italian Biographical and Bibliographical Encyclopedia*) are multi-volume sets containing biographical sketches of thousands of Italians who, from the Middle Ages to the twentieth century, distinguished themselves in the arts and humanities, in government, diplomacy, the military, science, education and other sectors of Italian life. Noting the places of origin of men and women with your family name —whether or not you can place them in your family tree—enables you to surmise where that surname predominated in Italy, and thereby defines the geographic limits of your research. Noting family names close to your own may help you to discover the original spelling of your surname. Besides, in searching such works, you may actually discover an ancestor or two of national prominence.

Genealogies of Italian Families.
Numerous published genealogies of Italian families may be found in American libraries with extensive genealogical collections, such as the New York Public Library and the Library of Congress. Such publications will not be of immediate use

to most Americans, however, for almost none of them chronicle the *popolino* (common people) who made up the bulk of emigrants to America. On the contrary, the vast majority of Italian genealogies document families of the aristocracy, nobility and royalty. They are usually large and sumptuous works published in the seventeenth, eighteenth and nineteenth centuries, sometimes illustrated with hand-colored coats-of-arms. The few Italians who do take an interest in family history tend to be titled men and women fascinated not only by the antiquity and honor of their heritage, but with heraldic art as well. *Contributo alla Bibliografia Genealogica Italiana* (*Contribution to Italian Genealogical Bibliography*), compiled by Antonio Gheno, is an extensive bibliography of published genealogies of ancient and illustrious families of Italy. *Albo Nazionale: Famiglie Nobili dello Stato Italiano* (*National Album: Noble Families of the Italian State*) is a dictionary of titled Italian families bearing arms. The *Libro d'Oro della Nobiltà Italiana* (*Golden Book of Italian Nobility*), updated every few years, is a directory of living Italians who hold titles.

(Hereditary titles have not been "recognized" in Italy since 1946 when the monarchy was abolished. All Italian citizens are equal under the law. Nevertheless, nobiliary titles continue to be used socially, and Italian courts have upheld the rights of noblemen against impostors who have usurped their titles. For a succinct explanation of Italian nobility, see "A Guide to Italian Heraldry" by Cav. (*Cavaliere*=knight=Sir) Louis Mendola in *POINTers*, Vol. 5, No. 4, Winter 1991.)

There are innumerable genealogies of the noble families of particular cities, such as Battilana's *Genealogie delle Famiglie Nobili di Genova* (*Genealogies of the Noble Families of Genoa*), and genealogies of the nobility of particular regions, such as Di Casalgerardo's *Nobiliario di Sicilia* (*Book of Nobility of Sicily*). If oral tradition has it that your family is a scion of a noble Italian house, published genealogies such as these, sooner or later in your research, may prove or disprove the claim. Even if your family has no such tradition, though, for the sake of thoroughness in your research, it is still wise to check published genealogies to see whether one with your surname exists. Family fortunes have been exhausted and "downward mobility" has been far from rare within the Italian nobility (see "Interpreting Italian Terms" in the Postcript at the end of this guide). American descendants of poor Italian immigrants do discover sometimes, after climbing a few generations of their family tree, that one branch or another does indeed link up with a noble or royal dynasty.

In addition, given the heightened interest in genealogy among Italian Americans today, you can never be sure that a distant cousin of yours living in another state, perhaps on the opposite side of the country, has not recently published something about your family. One recent and excellent example of an Italian-American family history is Sharon DeBartolo Carmack's *The Ebetino and Vallarelli Family History: Italian Immigrants to Westchester County, New York, in the Early 1900s, Including Descendants to 1990* (Anundsen Publishing Co., 1990). Though genealogical publishing is still young among Italian Americans, more such histories will be appearing in coming years.

Maps and Gazetteers. Maps of Italy and gazetteers of Italian towns are essential to consult because the internal and external boundaries of Italy have been redrawn many times over the centuries, and—as stated earlier—many towns and villages have the same or similar names. These towns and villages are also often clustered within a tight geographic area. The *Annuario Generale, Comuni e Frazioni d'Italia* (*General Annual, Townships and Villages of Italy*) is published every five years by the Touring Club Italiano of Milan. It lists all of the *comuni* (townships) and *frazioni* (villages) of Italy with essential data about each, including its province, current population, zip code, train station, parish, diocese and weekly market day. The *Nuovo Dizionario dei Comuni e Frazioni di Comuni* (*New Dictionary of Townships and Villages*), which is updated periodically, is another complete listing of Italy's *comuni* and *frazioni* giving the province in which each is located, with population figures and other administrative information. Use the facts you gathered from interviewing relatives and examining materials at home to determine which one of the several towns with the same name is your family's.

Until the end of World War I, the Austro-Hungarian Empire extended into a portion of what is today Italy. If your ancestor was born in a town of northern Italy whose name looks or sounds German, you may need to consult the gazetteer of the Austro-Hungarian Empire, *Allgemeines Geografisches Statistisches Lexikon aller Osterreichischen Staaten* (*General Geographical and Statistical Lexicon of All Austrian States*), to determine its location and, hence, its correct name today. This eleven-volume gazetteer is available on microfilm from the LDS FHL (see below).

Perhaps the most detailed atlas available for Italy is the *Grande Carta Topografica del Regno d'Italia* (*Great Topographical Map of the Kingdom of Italy*) printed by the *Istituto Geografico Militare* (Military Geographical Institute) in Florence beginning in 1882. It comprises the entire Italian peninsula, Sicily and Sardinia in 277 maps at a scale of 1:100,000, all of which were updated and republished periodically into the twentieth century. These maps show every topographical feature imaginable, including every hill, valley and river, every tiny cluster of houses, large orchards and vineyards, mines, railroads and railroad stations, all thoroughfares, from surfaced highways to footpaths, all bridges, substantial stone walls enclosing estates, convents and monasteries, ruins from antiquity, and more (see illustration on p. 45). Rural churches and cemeteries are marked, and villas in the countryside are often iden-

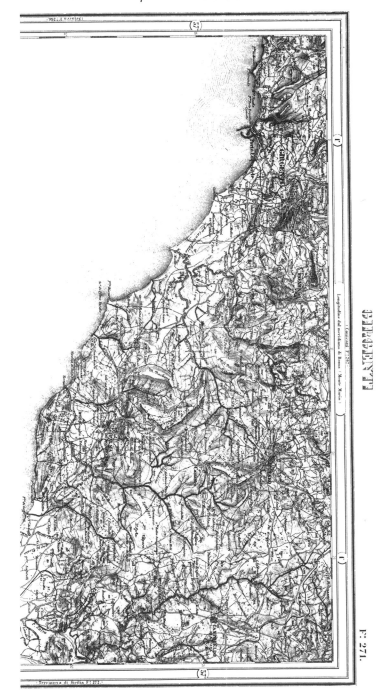

Portion of *Grande Carta Topografica* showing Sicilian coast east of the city of Girgenti. Note abundance of detail, including country houses labeled with the names of the families. (*Photocopy of original in the Library of Congress.*)

tified by family name. The Library of Congress has a complete set of the *Grande Carta Topografica del Regno d'Italia.*

Italian Local History. Just as there are published histories of American cities, counties and states, used by genealogists for the wealth of information they contribute to individual family histories, so too are there published histories of Italian towns, cities, provinces and regions which prove valuable to Americans researching their ancestry in Italy. Naturally, these are most often written in Italian by Italian historians, and are found in larger research libraries with extensive foreign collections, such as the Library of Congress and state and university libraries. They contain a wealth of detail about the families involved in the community's foundation and development, commercial activities, and social and religious life. For instance, *Casteldaccia nella Storia della Sicilia* (*Casteldaccia in the History of Sicily*) is a 295-page account of a tiny farming community from its earliest mention in seventeenth-century records to the mid-twentieth century. Researched and written by the pastor of the parish (the town only has one parish), this history indicates when each family first arrived, describes the composition and actions of the town council, and explains the community's involvement in larger historical events, such as the Risorgimento and World War I. The only way to know whether or not such a history exists for your ancestor's community is to search diligently with the help of librarians in larger research libraries.

More broadly accessible are histories of provinces and regions. *I Sette Re di Agrigento* (*The Seven Kings of Agrigento*), for example, not only relates the history of a Sicilian province, but includes a clear description of the organization and contents of the *archivio di stato* (state archives) in the provincial capital of Agrigento, and concludes with a list of the 688 *notai* (notaries) who worked in the notarial district of Agrigento between 1486 and 1859, and the 507 *notai* who worked in the notarial district of Sciacca between 1434 and 1875, with the years each was licensed. A work such as Giosue Musca's two-volume *Storia della Puglia* (*The History of Apulia*) covers the geographical, historical, political, social, economic and cultural development of an entire five-province *regione* (region). Provincial and regional histories do not provide the same amount of personal and familial detail that town histories do, though you may still find information about your ancestors if they participated in any way in provincial or regional affairs.

The Latter-day Saints Family History Library.
Besides these published resources in United States libraries, extensive and valuable materials made available through the LDS FHL can help you prepare thoroughly to find and use the Italian records of value for your family's story.

To learn what materials the LDS FHL holds, you consult its catalog. This can be done not only in Salt Lake City, but at LDS branch libraries—called family history centers—across the country and around the world, as well as at the Library of Congress and a few other major public libraries, such as the Chicago and Dallas Public Libraries. The catalog is in the form of a CD-ROM, which means you sit at a computer terminal, key in the names or topics of interest to you, and read the information that appears on the screen. The computer response will indicate whether or not any resources bearing on that name or topic are in the LDS FHL's collections. At many family history centers you may also consult the catalog in the form of microfiche. To use this, you consult a printed guide to the thousands of microfiche comprising the catalog, select by number the fiche that would appear to contain a name or subject useful for your research, and then view the fiche using a microfiche reader. You will see whether or not any resources on the name or topic you selected are in the LDS FHL.

After consulting the LDS FHL catalog, you may borrow any microfilm you think may further your research. Simply submit your request at any LDS family history center, pay a modest fee for postage, and the rolls of microfilm will be sent from Salt Lake City to the LDS family history center, where you may view it for a minimum period of three weeks before it is returned. Sometimes a six-month or indefinite loan period may be arranged.

For further information about the LDS FHL, its services, and the research publications it makes available for free or at a modest cost, write: Family History Library, North West Temple Street, Salt Lake City, UT 84150. Here is a brief summary of the LDS FHL's most important materials for Italian genealogy:

International Genealogical Index (IGI). The International Genealogical Index is a database that contains over 485,000 Italian names extracted from original birth and marriage records. An important part of preparing to use Italian records is to search the IGI for the surnames you will be researching in Italy. You may not find a single one of your ancestors in the IGI. On the other hand, you may find one or more, because the record of their birth or marriage happened to appear in a sacramental register selected for inclusion in the database. The IGI, therefore, is a tool which should not be overlooked, especially since it is constantly being expanded, and more and more Italian names appear in each new edition, the latest being 1992.

Microfilmed Italian Records. Since the early 1980s the LDS FHL has microfilmed millions of original records of genealogical value in Italian archives. An indispensable part of preparing to find and use Italian records, therefore—whether you intend to travel to Italy and do the research yourself, or correspond with the appropriate Italian record repositories for the information, or even hire a professional Italian genealogist—is to check the LDS FHL catalog *first* to see whether any records of your ancestral towns have been microfilmed. Even if you discover that the LDS FHL has not yet microfilmed any records of the towns where your ancestors lived, it is a good idea to borrow and examine several rolls of microfilmed records of any town in the general area where your ancestors lived. This serves two important and useful purposes: (1) it familiarizes you with the record sources available in Italy; and (2) it introduces you to the old script you will encounter in those Italian records (now your training in paleography begins!).

A useful tool for helping you decipher the Latin and Italian abbreviations you will encounter in the old civil and religious records of Italy is Cappelli's *Dizionario di Abbreviature Latine ed Italiane (Dictionary of Latin and Italian Abbreviations)* cited in the bibliography. In addition, the LDS FHL has published a *Genealogical Word List: Latin*, and a *Genealogical Word List: Italian*. These pamphlets contain the Latin and Italian words you are most likely to encounter in genealogical resources, and give their English translations.

Microfilmed Telephone Books. When searching for an ancestor's birthplace, it may be helpful to consult Italian telephone directories. For example, if you know the region where an ancestor was born, but not the exact province or town, you might consult a sampling of phone books from that region to see in which province or town your family name is concentrated, and then proceed to search in the records of that province or town as described in chapter 1. In Italy you will find a full set of telephone books in all airports and major train stations. A complete collection of Italian telephone directories is available on microfilm from the LDS FHL, and the Library of Congress has a set of originals. Or, if you prefer to buy one, you may do so from AT&T. Phone 1-800-538-2665, give the name of the locality of interest to you, and AT&T will quote a price and shipping charge and take your credit card order. For a check or money order purchase, send to: AT&T Foreign Directories, P.O. Box 19901, Indianapolis, IN 46219, ATTN: Commercial Sales.

Other Materials on Microfilm and in Computer Format. The LDS FHL also holds a wealth of other materials on microfilm or in computer format that are relevant to Italian genealogy. These include microfilm copies of many of the published works and federal, state and local records described earlier in the section headed "Where You Find These Three Basic Facts," as well as many of the resources—including maps and gazetteers—discussed in "Where You Find This Additional Information." For instance, the LDS FHL has a microfilm copy of the declarations of intention (for citizenship) made by Italian immigrants in the New York County Courthouse from 1897 through 1906, as well as an index to them. It has on compact disc a Social Security Death Index that lists 1.5 million persons who had Social Security numbers and whose deaths were reported to the Social Security Administration between 1937 and 1962, and 38 million persons whose deaths were reported between 1962 and 1988 (see the article by Sharon DeBartolo Carmack cited in the bibliography). It has on microfilm state censuses for all states that made separate enumerations. It also has a spotty collection of several old Italian serials which focus on aristocratic, noble and royal genealogy and heraldry. In short, many of the resources discussed above are readily available on microfilm through the LDS FHL. It should not be overlooked.

Institutions and Journals. There are several major research centers in the United States that hold substantial collections of materials relating to Italian immigration and Italian-American history. The Immigration History Research Center at the University of Minnesota in St. Paul contains an Italian-American collection comprising about

1,400 items, including not only standard published works in the field of Italian immigration history, but unpublished dissertations too, and many books, tracts and pamphlets printed in Italian by immigrant presses. The archives of the Order of the Sons of Italy in America are also a part of this collection. For guides to the Italian-American collection in the Immigration History Research Center, see the "Research Aids" section of the bibliography. (Genealogical institutions in Italy are discussed in chapter 3.)

The Italian Genealogical Society of America was founded in 1994 (P.O. Box 8571, Cranston, RI 02920-8571) to help Italian Americans research and preserve their heritage. The Society publishes a quarterly newsletter and holds several meetings during the year.

The Augustan Society, based in Torrance, California, publishes an occasional journal titled, *The Italian Genealogist.* It is edited by the Very Reverend Lawrence Casati, one of the very few American-born professional genealogists based in Italy.

Only one American journal published regularly is devoted exclusively to Italian genealogical research: *POINTers* (Pursuing Our Italian Names Together). This quarterly is an informal vehicle for the exchange among its subscribers of information about resources and methods for Italian genealogy. One asset of *POINTers* is that it reprints, when permission is granted, articles about Italian genealogy which have appeared in other publications, making the journal a kind of "clearing house" of information about Italian-American family research. The *POINTers* data bank of Italian surnames being researched by its subscribers may alert you to the fact that a relative is already working on some branch of your family tree.

Now, having exploited the Italian record sources available in the United States, you are thoroughly prepared to continue your research in record sources in Italy.

1. Civil Record Repositories in Italy

Whether conducting your research in person or through correspondence, you should be familiar with the civil archives in Italy—their organizational structure as well as their holdings. Italy is divided into twenty administrative *regioni* (see map of contemporary Italy on pp. 54–55, but no records are kept on the regional level. Each *regione* contains from one to eleven *provincie*, with a total of 103 *provincie* in all. Each *provincia* contains many *comuni*, one of which serves as the provincial capital. The name of the province and the name of its capital are the same. Some Italian communities are so small that they do not have their own mayor, but rather fall within the administrative jurisdiction of a *comune;* these are called *frazioni di comuni,* or simply *frazioni.*

There are ninety-five *archivi di stato:* one *archivio di stato* in almost every provincial capital (94 out of 103), plus the *Archivio Centrale dello Stato* (Central State Archives) in Rome. Some *archivi di stato* have a *sezione* (department or branch) in one or two smaller cities of the province, when the local collections are large enough to warrant such a *sezione.* Besides these *archivi di stato,* local *archivi comunali* (town archives) are kept in every *municipio* (town hall).

The *Guida Generale degli Archivi di Stato Italiani* (*General Guide to the Italian State Archives*) is the official and definitive guide to Italian archives published in four volumes by

Contemporary Italy. *(Drawn by the author.)*

CONTEMPORARY ITALY

*(Each province is listed with its abbreviation and
the first two digits of its five-digit postal code)*

I. ABRUZZO
1. Chieti (CH, 66)
2. L'Aquila (AQ, 67)
3. Pescara (PE, 65)
4. Teramo (TE, 64)

II. BASILICATA
5. Matera (MT, 75)
6. Potenza (PZ, 85)

III. CALABRIA
7. Catanzaro (CZ, 88)
8. Cosenza (CS, 87)
9. Crotone (KR, 88)
10. Reggio Calabria (RC, 89)
11. Vibo Valentia (VV, 88)

IV. CAMPANIA
12. Avellino (AV, 83)
13. Benevento (BN, 82)
14. Caserta (CE, 81)
15. Napoli = Naples (NA, 80)
16. Salerno (SA, 84)

V. EMILIA-ROMAGNA
17. Bologna (BO, 40)
18. Ferrara (FE, 44)
19. Forli (FO, 47)
20. Modena (MO, 41)
21. Parma (PR, 43)
22. Piacenza (PC, 29)
23. Ravenna (RA, 48)
24. Reggio Emilia (RE, 42)
25. Rimini (RN, 47)

VI. FRIULI-VENEZIA GIULIA
26. Gorizia (GO, 34)
27. Pordenone (PN, 33)
28. Trieste (TS, 34)
29. Udine (UD, 33)

VII. LAZIO = LATIUM
30. Frosinone (FR, 03)
31. Latina (LT, 04)
32. Rieti (RI, 02)
33. Roma = Rome (ROMA, 00)
34. Viterbo (VT, 01)

VIII. LIGURIA
35. Genova = Genoa (GE, 16)
36. Imperia (IM, 18)
37. La Spezia (SP, 19)
38. Savona (SV, 17)

IX. LOMBARDIA = LOMBARDY
39. Bergamo (BG, 24)
40. Brescia (BS, 25)
41. Como (CO, 22)
42. Cremona (CR, 26)
43. Lecco (LC, 22)
44. Lodi (LO, 20)
45. Mantova (MN, 46)
46. Milano = Milan (MI, 20)
47. Pavia (PV, 27)
48. Sondrio (SO, 23)
49. Varese (VA, 21)

X. MARCHE
50. Ancona (AN, 60)
51. Ascoli Piceno (AP, 63)
52. Macerata (MC, 62)

53. Pesaro-Urbino (PS, 61)

XI. MOLISE
54. Campobasso (CB, 86)
55. Isernia (IS, 86)

XII. PIEMONTE = PIEDMONT
56. Alessandria (AL, 15)
57. Asti (AT, 14)
58. Biella (BI, 13)
59. Cuneo (CN, 12)
60. Novara (NO, 28)
61. Torino = Turin (TO, 10)
62. Verbano-Cusio-Ossola (VB, 28)
63. Vercelli (VC, 13)

XIII. PUGLIA = APULIA
64. Bari (BA, 70)
65. Brindisi (BR, 72)
66. Foggia (FG, 71)
67. Lecce (LE, 73)
68. Taranto (TA, 74)

XIV. SARDEGNA = SARDINIA
69. Cagliari (CA, 09)
70. Nuoro (NU, 08)
71. Oristano (OR, 09)
72. Sassari (SS, 07)

XV. SICILIA = SICILY
73. Agrigento (AG, 92)
74. Caltanissetta (CL, 93)
75. Catania (CT, 95)
76. Enna (EN, 94)
77. Messina (ME, 98)
78. Palermo (PA, 90)
79. Ragusa (RG, 97)
80. Siracusa (SR, 96)
81. Trapani (TP, 91)

XVI. TOSCANA = TUSCANY
82. Arezzo (AR, 52)
83. Firenze = Florence (FI, 50)
84. Grosseto (GR, 58)
85. Livorno = Leghorn (LI, 57)
86. Lucca (LU, 55)
87. Massa Carrara (MS, 54)
88. Pisa (PI, 56)
89. Pistoia (PT, 51)
90. Prato (PO, 50)
91. Siena (SI, 53)

XVII. TRENTINO-ALTO ADIGE
92. Bolzano (BZ, 39)
93. Trento (TN, 38)

XVIII. UMBRIA
94. Perugia (PG, 06)
95. Terni (TR, 05)

XIX. VALLE D'AOSTA
96. Aosta (AO, 11)

XX. VENETO
97. Belluno (BL, 32)
98. Padova = Padua (PD, 35)
99. Rovigo (RO, 45)
100. Treviso (TV, 31)
101. Venezia = Venice (VE, 30)
102. Verona (VR, 37)
103. Vicenza (VI, 36)

the *Ministero per i Beni Culturali e Ambientali* (Ministry of Cultural and Environmental Affairs), the government agency responsible for administration of the archives and libraries of Italy. Taking the *archivi di stato* in alphabetical order, this guide describes each one's holdings. Every description includes a section titled *"Archivi di Famiglie e di Persone"* ("Personal and Family Archives") which lists the personal papers that are deposited in the archives. These manuscript collections contain substantial genealogical and biographical information about individual Italian families.

The *Ministero per i Beni Culturali e Ambientali* also publishes a set of twenty modest monographs under the colorful title of *Itinerari Archivistici Italiani* (*Italian Archival Itineraries*). The first—*Organizzazione Archivistica* (*Archival Organization*)—describes the national archival system. The second—*Archivio Centrale dello Stato*—describes the central archives in Rome. Each of the eighteen others describes the *archivi di stato* located in each *regione* of Italy (Abruzzo and Molise are combined into one, and there appears to be none, as of this writing, for the Valle D'Aosta). These superbly illustrated little volumes present a brief overview of the documentary materials in each archives, plus all of the essential practical information regarding addresses, hours of operation, photocopying services, and so forth, you would need to know to use the archives.

A third reference work that can prove invaluable for your genealogical research in Italy is the *Guida Monaci: Annuario Generale Italiano* (*Monaci Guide: General Italian Annual*). This weighty tome, updated every year, is a directory of all of Italy's governmental offices and agencies. It lists every public archives and library in the country, with its address, phone number and the name of its director.

The civil records described below vary widely not only in the accuracy, amount and type of information they contain, but in their physical condition as well. Italy as a modern nation is young; it was unified from numerous independent states during the 1860s, and only became a single country with its capital at Rome in 1870. Prior to that time, "Italy" was composed of city states and principalities in the north, with a tradition of Austrian influence; the Papal States in the center; and in the south, the Kingdom of the Two Sicilies, ruled by Bourbon monarchs in Naples. Customs, traditions and language varied markedly from one geographic area to the next. (See map of pre-unification Italy on pp. 58–59.) Each of these states experienced different wars and natural disasters and changes in leadership and administration, and each kept its records in its own way. Naturally, therefore, no record description could possibly hold true universally throughout Italy.

It was Napoleon Bonaparte who, during his brief dominion over the affairs of Italy from 1806 to 1815, unified the administrative, judicial and legislative system of the entire country into one substantially similar to the system of *regioni*, *provincie* and *comuni* described above. (Napoleone Buonaparte, who later "Frenchified" his name, was born of Italian parentage in Ajaccio, Corsica, in 1769.) Though Italy was restored to its pre-Napoleonic autonomous states by the Congress of Vienna in 1815, the Emperor's system of *regioni*, *provincie*, *comuni* and *frazioni* remained the model for modern-day Italy. By 1860 King Vittorio Emanuele II of Piedmont had emerged as the champion of Italian unification. Between 1860 and 1865, Garibaldi and his Redshirts, devoted subjects of Vittorio Emanuele, captured Sicily and Naples for their king. In 1866, as a result of war with Austria, the king also gained Venice as part of his realm. Finally, in 1870, Italy as a united country, with Rome as its capital city, was born—though a *de jure* state of war continued to exist between the Kingdom of Italy and the Papal State (reduced by this time to the Vatican) until the Lateran Treaty of 1929. (For more information about the history and formation of Italy, see the "General Histories of Italy" section of the bibliography.) The following descriptions of Italian civil records, therefore, are helpful generalizations, and

Pre-Unification Italy. *(Drawn by the author.)*

PRE-UNIFICATION ITALY (1859)

REGNO DI SARDEGNA =
KINGDOM OF SARDINIA

   PIEMONTE = PIEDMONT
1. Alessandria
2. Anneci
3. Aosta
4. Coni
5. Genova
6. Nizza
7. Novara
8. Savoia
9. Savona
10. Torino
11. Vercelli

   SARDEGNA = SARDINIA
12. Cagliari
13. Nuoro
14. Sassari

LOMBARDIA-VENEZIA =
LOMBARDY-VENICE
15. Belluno
16. Bergamo
17. Brescia
18. Como
19. Cremona
20. Lodi
21. Mantova
22. Milano
23. Padova
24. Pavia
25. Polesina
26. Sondrio
27. Treviso
28. Udine
29. Venezia
30. Verona
31. Vicenza

PARMA

MODENA

LUCCA

TOSCANA = TUSCANY
32. Arezzo
33. Firenze
34. Grossetto
35. Pisa
36. Siena

STATI DELLA CHIESA =
PAPAL STATES
37. Ancona
38. Ascoli
39. Bologna
40. Camerino
41. Civita Vecchia
42. Fermo
43. Ferrara
44. Forli
45. Frosinone
46. Macerata
47. Orvieto
48. Perugia
49. Ravenna
50. Rieti
51. Roma
52. Spoleto
53. Urbino & Pesaro
54. Velletri
55. Viterbo

REGNO DELLE DUE SICILIE =
KINGDOM OF THE TWO SICILIES

   NAPOLI = NAPLES
56. Abbruzzo Citra
57. Abbruzzo Ultra 1
58. Abbruzzo Ultra 2
59. Basilicata
60. Calabria Citra
61. Calabria Ultra
62. Capitanata
63. Molise
64. Napoli
65. Principato Citra
66. Principato Ultra
67. Terra di Bari
68. Terra di Lavoro
69. Terra d'Otranto

   SICILIA = SICILY
70. Caltanisetta
71. Catania
72. Girgenti
73. Messina
74. Palermo
75. Siragosa
76. Trapani

Americans seeking their ancestors in Italy will soon discover just how much these descriptions may vary from the norm in any particular locality and era.

Archivio Comunale (Town Archives)

It makes sense to begin a description of Italian records on the local level because most Italian records of genealogical value are maintained by the town or city—that is, by the *comune*. It is usually in the *municipio* of your immigrant ancestor's native *comune* that your family research in Italian civil records will begin.

According to Italian law, the registers comprising the *archivio comunale* may only be searched by an official working in the *municipio*. Just how much searching and reporting such an official will perform for an American—who either writes or shows up in person—varies widely not only from one *comune* to another, but from one clerk to another in the same *municipio*. Some are more cooperative and helpful than others. On occasion an American who speaks directly to the clerk's superior—the *ufficiale dello stato civile* himself or the *"direttore"* (director)—may be allowed to search through the registers himself, one register at a time. But this happy scenario is very rare. The more specific and accurate the information you provide, the better the chances you will receive a positive reaction from the clerk. It is good to keep in mind that a town hall is a functioning public office and is neither intended nor staffed to render assistance to historical researchers.

Stato Civile. Birth, marriage and death records, called *stato civile* (vital records), have been kept uniformly throughout Italy since 1870. (Earlier *stato civile* for some *regioni* will be discussed under **Archivio di Stato** below.) They are maintained by the *Ufficio di Stato Civile* (Office of Vital Statistics) in the *municipio* and are rich in family information.

Atto di Nascita. To create an *Atto di Nascita* (birth record) the infant—usually less than one day old—had to be presented physically—usually by the father—to the town's *ufficiale dello stato civile* (recorder of vital records), who was usually the *sindaco* (mayor). The record contains the date of the presentation at the town hall; name, age, profession and place of residence of the presenter; the maiden name, age and place of residence of the mother; the name, age, profession and place of residence of the father; the date, hour and place of birth of the infant, and his or her name; and the names, ages, professions and places of residence of two witnesses to the presentation (see illustration on pp. 62–63). In many localities of Italy this information is written on the left side of the page, and on the right side is a brief record of the infant's baptism—usually occurring the same day or the next—which gives only the date and parish of the baptism.

A child whose father is given as *padre ignoto* (father unknown) and whose mother is given as *madre ignota* (mother unknown) was usually a foundling. Obviously, unless some tradition about the birth is passed on orally within the family, tracing the parentage of such a foundling may be impossible. A child whose mother's name is recorded, but whose father is given as *padre ignoto*, was often an illegitimate child.

Sometimes, when a person married or died in a *comune* other than his or her native *comune*, the *ufficiale dello stato civile* recording the event would forward the information to the *ufficiale dello stato civile* in the *comune* of birth, who in turn would annotate the original *atto di nascita*. This practice has been observed with varying regularity across the country and across the years.

Atto della Solenne Promessa di Celebrare il Matrimonio. A marriage record is called an *Atto della Solenne Promessa di Celebrare il Matrimonio* (Record of the Solemn Promise to Celebrate Matrimony), because the marriage itself was not

First page of a typical 2-page *atto di nascita*, recording the birth of Rosa Fascella, daughter of Gaetano Fascella and Domenica Benigno, on 21 October 1829 in the *comune* of Misilmeri, *provincia* of Palermo. (*Photograph courtesy of the Latter-day Saints Family History Library.*)

Page from a typical index found at the end of a register of births, showing that the record of "Fascella Rosa," born 21 October 1829, of Fascella Gaetano and Benigno Domenica is record number 153 in the register. (*Photograph courtesy of the Latter-day Saints Family History Library.*)

ATTO DELLA SOLENNE PROMESSA Di celebrare il Matrimonio	Indicazione della seguita celebrazione Canonica del Matrimonio
Num. d' ordine *ventuno* L' anno *1824* il dì *dieci del — mese di ottobre* — alle ore *sedici* — avanti di noi *Luigi Raitano Eletto* ed ufficiale dello stato civile del Comune di *Bagheria* Distretto di *Palermo* Valle di *Palermo* sono comparsi nella casa comunale *Leopo. Di Girgenti* di anni *ventinove* nato in *Palermo* Distretto di *Palermo* Valle di *Palermo* di professione *Caffettiere* — domiciliato in *Bagheria* figlio di *D. Giovanni* di anni — di professione *praticante* domiciliato in *Palermo* e della *fu Francesca Piola* di anni — domiciliata *in detta* — e *D'Eia Supralmonde* di anni *vero sei* — nata in *Palermo* domiciliata *in Bagheria* figlia di *maggio Cosimo* di anni — di professione *Bottaro* domiciliato *in Bagheria* e della *fu M. La vanna Savona* di anni — domiciliata *in detta* — i quali alla presenza de' testimonj, che saranno qui appresso indicati, e da essi prodotti, ci hanno richiesto di ricevere la loro solenne promessa di celebrare avanti alla Chiesa secondo le forme prescritte dal Sacro	Num. d' ordine *ventuno* L' anno *1824* il dì *ventitrè* del mese di *ottobre* Il Parroco di *Bagheria* — ci ha rimessa una delle copie della controscritta promessa ; in piè della quale ha certificato, che la celebrazione del matrimonio è seguita nel giorno *ventidue* del mese di *Sopra* — anno *sudetto* alla presenza de' testimonj In vista di essa, noi abbiamo disteso il presente notamento, e dopo di averla cifrata, abbiamo disposto, che fosse la copia anzidetta conservata nel volume de' documenti al foglio Abbiamo inoltre accusato al Parroco la ricezione della medesima ed abbiamo sottoscritto il presente atto, ch'è stato inscritto su i due registri . *Luigi Raitano*

First page of a typical 4-page *atto della solenne promessa,* recording the marriage of Don Leopoldo Girgenti and Donna Giuseppa LoMonaco on 10 October 1824 in the *comune* of Bagheria, *provincia* of Palermo. (*Photograph courtesy of the Latter-day Saints Family History Library.*)

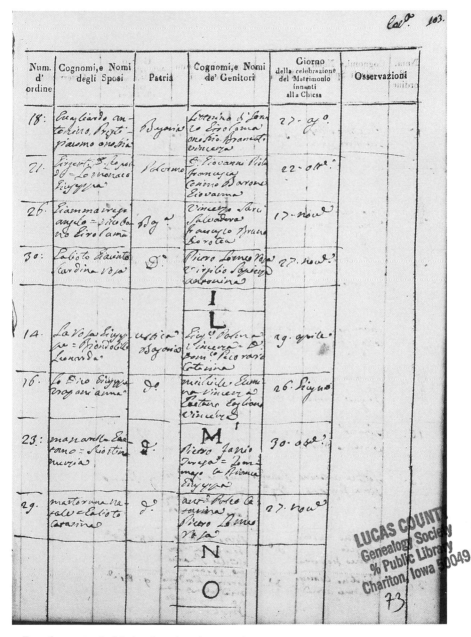

Page from a typical index found at the end of a register of marriages, showing that the record for "Girgenti, D. Leopoldo = LoMonaco, D. Giuseppa" is record number 21 in the register. (*Photograph courtesy of the Latter-day Saints Family History Library.*)

contracted at city hall, but rather in the religious ceremony which followed in the church. To create an *Atto della Solenne Promessa* the bride and groom would appear before the *ufficiale dello stato civile* with four witnesses. The record contains the date of the appearance at the town hall; name, age, birthplace, profession and place of residence of the groom, together with his father's name, age, profession and place of residence, and his mother's maiden name, age and place of residence; the name, age, birthplace and place of residence of the bride, together with her father's name, age, profession and place of residence, and her mother's maiden name, age and place of residence; and the names, ages, professions and places of residence of the four witnesses (see illustration on pp. 64–65). If the groom is a widower, or the bride is a widow, this will be stated also, sometimes with the name of the former spouse. Those principals present who could write signed their names at the end of the record. In many localities of Italy this information is written on the left side of the page, and the right side contains a brief record of the sacramental union which followed in the church, containing only the date and parish of the marriage.

Atto di Morto. An *Atto di Morto* (death record) is very brief. It provides the name and age of the deceased, and the date and place of death. Sometimes it will also give the deceased person's occupation, residence, name of last spouse, and parents' names. The death record of a married woman lists her under her maiden name, *not* her husband's surname.

The *stato civile* just described are usually kept in volumes by year, and most volumes are indexed in the back. Some have ten-year cumulative indexes.

Certificato di Residenza. Another record maintained in the *municipio* of great value to genealogists is the *Certificato di Residenza* (Certificate of Residency). This is a record of where a family resides in the *comune*, and of any changes in residency—to another address, for example, or to another *comune* of Italy, or to a foreign country. The *certificato di residenza*, therefore, may show your ancestor's exact year of emigration to America. All citizens of Italy carry a *carta d'identità* (identification card) which gives their legal address. When issuing such a *carta d'identità*, the local official checks the *Certificato di Residenza*.

Certificato di Stato di Famiglia. A third record, which appears to be peculiar to Italy, is the *Certificato di Stato di Famiglia* (Certificate of Family Status). This is obtained from the *Ufficio di Anagrafe* (Office of the Census) in the *municipio*. A *certificato di stato di famiglia* shows the composition of a family unit, including the names, relationships, birth dates and birthplaces of all members living when the record was made. The certificate may also show marriage and death dates added to the record as the events occurred. This distinctively Italian record reflects the desire and effort of each *comune* to maintain an on-going account of the status of each of its families. Although some towns have kept this type of record since 1870, it was rare prior to 1911.

Archivio di Stato (State Archives)

After *archivi comunali*, the record repository of greatest value for genealogical information is the *archivio di stato* in the capital city of the province where your ancestors lived.

Archivi di stato are public archives staffed by archivists and trained clerks who are prepared to help you access the records you seek. The professional staff cannot, however, be expected to conduct research for you, either by correspondence or in person. Limited funds, time and personnel preclude that. They will respond to queries about their institution's holdings, but will not do any searching for you in the collections. That's *your* job! Access to Italy's *archivi di stato* is free to all researchers for historic purposes; researchers working on commercial projects, however, must pay a fee and obtain a written permit. Practically all *archivi di stato* have their own photocopying and microfilming services, or can provide such services through approved private agencies for a reasonable fee. The bureaucratic obstacle course the researcher must negotiate to access these services, though, may seem maddeningly convoluted and exasperating to Americans.

In the Mezzogiorno, *archivi di stato* may conserve not only the civil records described below, but some of the religious records described in chapter 2. This is because substantial Church property was confiscated and "secularized" by the new government following Garibaldi's conquest in 1860. Since that time there has been a certain tension between some ecclesiastical and civil authorities regarding the restoration of Church records to their original repositories. The struggle waxes and wanes, depending on the character and determination of the officials in office at any given moment, but seems never to be definitively resolved. *Archivi di stato* north of Naples may also hold a variety of religious records.

Stato Civile. The *Archivio di Stato* contains *stato civile* kept prior to 1870. It was in 1806 that Napoleon Bonaparte decreed that all births, marriages and deaths be registered with civil authorities throughout the country. In northern Italy the keeping of *stato civile* was initiated anywhere between 1806 and 1815. After the Congress of Vienna in 1815, however, when Italy reverted to its pre-Napoleonic status, some areas of the north discontinued keeping *stato civile* until 1870. In the central Italian *regione* of Toscana, the *stato civile* housed in the *Archivio di Stato* in Florence is continuous since 1808. In the southern *regioni* of Abruzzo, Molise, Campania, Puglia, Basilicata, Calabria, and Sicilia—which once comprised the Kingdom of the Two Sicilies—

stato civile were kept continuously from 1809 on the mainland and from 1820 in Sicily. All of the pre-1870 *stato civile* kept in *archivi di stato* are similar in form and content to those housed in the *archivi comunali* described above, and most were microfilmed during the 1980s by the LDS FHL.

The northern *regione* of Trentino-Alto Adige, comprised of the *provincie* of Bolzano and Trento, was under Austrian control prior to Italian unification in 1870. The custom there since the sixteenth century was for the local priest to serve as the *ufficiale dello stato civile* for his *comune*. Pre-1870 *stato civile* for Bolzano and Trento, therefore, may still be found in the custody of local priests, rather than in the *archivi di stato*.

Allegati. In a few provinces—especially in the Kingdom of the Two Sicilies, but never in the north—an additional record source may be found among the pre-1870 *stato civile: allegati* or *processi matrimoniali* (annexed documents). *Allegati* are documents presented by the bride and groom when recording their *solenne promessa* in the *municipio*. Hence, they are kept in a separate volume in connection with (annexed to) the *atti di matrimonio*. *Allegati* usually include: birth or baptismal certificates for the two spouses; death certificates when one or more of the spouse's parents was deceased; and records of previous marriages, and of the death of previous spouses, of the bride and groom. Such *allegati* are in volumes separate from the *atti di matrimonio*, and have not been microfilmed by the LDS FHL. Nevertheless, it is evident how valuable they could be for your research, if indeed your ancestors resided in one of the southern provinces where *processi matrimoniali* were kept.

Registri degli Uffici di Leva. Shortly after the unification of Italy, military service became mandatory for all twenty-year-old males. Since about 1870, therefore, *registri degli Uffici di Leva* (registers of the Offices of Conscription) have been kept. These *registri* list the name, *comune* of birth, date of birth, parents' names, and physical description of all young men eligible for the draft, together with an explanation of their military status—whether they ever

served, or deserted, or were exempted, and so forth. The *registri* are divided into annual *classe di leva* (conscription classes or groups), each of which is indexed by the names of the draftees who composed that *classe di leva*—that is, the names of those who turned twenty since the previous *classe di leva*. *Registri degli Uffici di Leva* are maintained by *Distretto Militare* (Military District)—a *provincia* may contain perhaps five or six *distretti militare*—and those created since World War I may still be in the custody of the *Distretto Militare* where they were created. But older *registri di leva* have been deposited in the *archivio di stato.*

If you know your ancestor's *comune* of birth, and you wish to search for his military record, consult the *Nuovo Dizionario dei Comuni e Frazioni di Comuni* (see bibliography) to learn which *distretto militare* had jurisdiction over his *comune*. This will reduce the number of registers you will need to search to those of a single *distretto militare*. Note, too, that draftee records may sometimes be found on the township level; so if you know your ancestor's birthplace you might be able to find a record of his military status in the *archivio comunale* there.

However, if all you know is your ancestor's *provincia*, *registri di leva* may be an especially valuable resource, for they contain his *comune* of birth. Search the indexes of all the *classe di leva* most likely to include your ancestor in all of the registers of the five or six *distretti militare* of your ancestor's *provincia*. If you are seeking the birthplace of a female ancestor, you may search the indexes for her father's name or brother's name. This may be time-consuming, but the draft record you eventually find will yield your ancestral *comune* of origin. Knowing only an ancestor's *regione*, though, is an insufficient basis for undertaking a search of *registri di leva*, or any other Italian record.

Earlier records of military service, dating back sometimes to the late eighteenth century and containing more or less the same information as the *registri di leva*, are also kept in *archivi di stato*. These records cover the different Italian states and kingdoms at different periods of history, those of the *regione* of Tuscany being notably plentiful. Whether or not you find one pertaining to your ancestor will depend on many factors.

Minute, Atti e Bastardelli Notarili. Notaries have always been much more important and have always performed a much broader scope of legal services in Italy than in the United States. Italian law requires that marriage contracts and dowries, wills, real and personal property transactions, lawsuits of all kinds, including settlements of heirship and guardianship of orphans, and still other matters, be officially registered by a *notaio* (notary). From the Middle Ages through the early twentieth century, the *notaio*'s professional activity remained substantially unchanged and resulted in three different records of value to genealogists: *minute, atti* and *bastardelli*.

When the notary met with his clients, he wrote a *minuta* (rough draft) of the transaction to be recorded, including the names of the principals and the facts of the matter at hand. From his *minuta* he prepared the actual *atto* (deed), which is the written record of the transaction. The notary kept his *minuta* and a copy of the *atto* for his own records, but deposited the original *atto* in the office of the *distretto notarile* (notarial district) where he was licensed. The deed was then considered legally registered.

For his own purposes the notary maintained a chronological list of the *atti* he prepared, with a few words defining the parameters of each *atto*. This list—known as *"bastardelli"* because the abstracts were "illegitimate;" that is, they did not constitute a legal document—provided accessibility for the notary to his own work. When a notary retired, or died, his *minute* and *bastardelli* were usually passed on to his successor. When the new notary found he

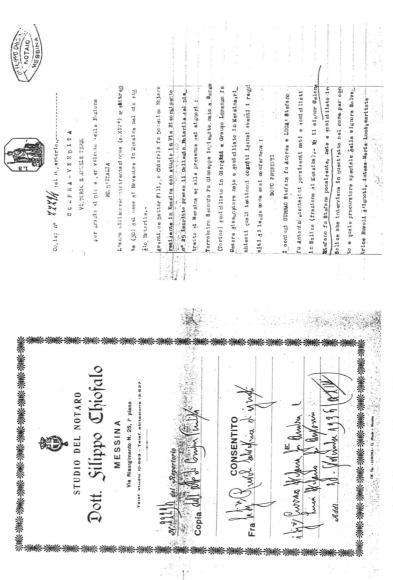

First two pages of an Italian notarial record dated 30 November 1935. The language and content of this deed of land transfer hardly vary from comparable notarial records of earlier centuries. (*From the collection of Louis Chibbaro.*)

had no further need of these, he deposited them in the office of his *distretto notarile.*

Notarial records of the past 100 years are still found in the possession of the individual notaries, or in the files of district notarial offices, or in archives—such as the *Archivio Notarile Distrettuale di Napoli* (District Notarial Archives of Naples)—which some populous notarial districts have had to create specifically for that purpose (see illustration on p. 72). At the end of 100 years, however, the whole collection of *minute, atti* and *bastardelli* described above is transferred to the *archivio di stato.* These notarial records in *archivi di stato* may date back to the fourteenth century and sometimes even earlier.

In the *archivio di stato,* each notary's archives forms a separate collection, and the *bastardelli* serve as a kind of index to the collection. But remember, the *bastardelli* list the *atti* in chronological order and do *not* constitute a name index to the *atti.* In addition, the original *atti* which were deposited in the district notarial office by all of the notaries licensed in that district—perhaps fifty to eighty notaries— are also gathered into separate collections, one for each notary. These collections are arranged in chronological order by the registration date of each *atto, not* the date when the transaction occurred, and *not* by the names of the principals or the content of the *atto.* Therefore, if you do not know the name of the notary engaged by your ancestors to register their legal transactions, or at least an approximate date when any particular record you seek was registered, researching notarial records may be very time-consuming, as a page-by-page search through the collections of all of the notaries of a given district is required.

Depending on your research needs, however, the time may turn out to be wisely spent and may result in a wealth of information about the social and economic status of your ancestors. By their nature, notarial records are full of familial matters, relationships and dates, so that in some cases—when civil or religious records are lacking—they may be the only resource available for establishing a family group. To ignore them would be tantamount to ignoring the wealth of comparable records that fill county court-houses throughout the United States.

It is far from an easy task, however, to decipher the content of early notarial records once you have found them! They were written in a Latin jargon with its own abbreviations, in a compact script called *gotico notarile* (notarial gothic). Unless your skills as a paleographer have been finely honed by this time in your research, you will have to hire a professional genealogist to decipher the notarial records for you. In rare and fortunate instances you may find notarial records that have been edited by scholars and printed in volumes specifically for historical research purposes. For example, in the *Archivio di Stato* in Trapani is the oldest register kept by an identified notary in Sicily. In 1943 it was transcribed into modern Italian, analyzed and published as *Il Registro Notarile di Giovanni Maiorana, 1297–1300 (The Notarial Register of Giovanni Maiorana, 1297–1300)* by the historian Antonino de Stefano (see bibliography). This volume is now available in the *biblioteca comunale* (municipal library) in Erice, the town near Trapani where the notary lived, as well as other Italian libraries and the New York Public Library.

Notary records kept in Jewish communities throughout Italy are being edited and published by Shlomo Simonsohn (see the bibliography and chapter 2), and notary records kept in the Waldensian communities of Piedmont are available in the *Archivio di Stato* in Turin (see chapter 2).

These happy exceptions notwithstanding, most notarial records are *not* transcribed into modern Italian and are *not* conveniently published in book form. Deciphering them requires considerable skill . . . and considerable patience.

Censimenti. National *censimenti* (censuses) of Italy taken in 1861, 1871, 1881, 1891 and 1901 are available for searching in *archivi di stato*. Later censuses of 1911—considered the first major national census—1921, 1931, 1936, 1951, 1961, 1971 and 1981 are not open to the public. *Censimenti* are enumerations of the total population of Italy by family unit, including the names and ages of the husband, wife and dependent children, occupation of the head of household, and places of birth of all members of the family.

Many *archivi di stato* also hold an assortment of other censuses taken at various times in various localities. These date back to the middle of the eighteenth century and show substantially the same information as the later censuses. For example, censuses were taken in the *regione* of *Sardegna* (Sardinia) in 1848 and 1857. For years prior to about 1750, however, you must turn to parish censuses (described below under *"Archivi Parrocchiali"*) or to *catasti* (tax lists) for enumerations of family units.

Catasti. Italians have lived with a wide variety of tax obligations over the centuries, from taxes on land and houses to taxes on livestock and family members, and more. *Catasti* (tax assessment records or lists), therefore, are varied and voluminous. They enumerate property owners—sometimes including the names, or the names and ages, of the property owner's household—and indicate the taxable property and amount of tax assessed on it. They may be civil records or parish tithing records. They may date back as far as the fourteenth century or be as recent as the nineteenth century.

Some *catasti* are called *Riveli* (*Declarations*), which consist of lists of heads of household "declaring" or "revealing" the precise extent and nature of the taxable property they hold, including *beni mobili* (personal property) and *beni immobili* (real estate). *Riveli* are particularly useful because they include names of members of each taxpayer's household. However, they are also voluminous and require a time-consuming page-by-page search.

Catasti pertaining to the former Papal States—the present-day provinces of Ancona, Ascoli Piceno, Macerata and Pesaro-Urbino (the region of *Marche*), Perugia and Terni (the region of *Umbria*), and Frosinone, Latina, Rieti, Roma and Viterbo (the region of *Lazio*)—are not kept in their respective *archivi di stato*, but rather in the *Archivio Segreto del Vaticano* (Secret Archives of the Vatican).

Catasti are especially useful sources of information about families that owned land, no matter how little. Ownership of modest pieces of private land was historically much more common north of Naples than in the Mezzogiorno, where most of the land was divided into huge *latifondi* (large estates) owned by a few noble families. As a result of this ancient feudal system, the vast majority of people in the south were landless peasants living and working on their titled landlord's *latifondo*. Nevertheless, persons without real estate could still appear in *catasti* prepared for taxing personal estate, such as a "head tax" on members of the family. *Catasti*, unfortunately—like notary records—are a difficult resource to use, since they are multifarious and written in arcane script and unindexed.

Registri dell'Emigrazione e Passaporti. The few Italians who emigrated to the American colonies in the seventeenth and eighteenth centuries sailed mostly from England or Holland in English or Dutch sailing vessels. By the mid-nineteenth century, however, when both Italian emigration to the United States and the use of steam-powered ships were on the rise, emigrants were beginning to sail directly out of Italian ports on Italian steamships. Genoa, Trieste, Naples, and Palermo quickly became the busiest ports of departure. Emigrants tended to use the port most accessible to their *comune*: those who lived in the north generally favored Genoa, though residents of the

northeast might use Trieste instead; those who lived in the Mezzogiorno used Naples and Palermo.

However, do not assume that because your ancestors were Italian they emigrated to the United States directly from Italian ports or sailed on Italian liners. By the twentieth century the French ports of Marseilles and LeHavre were also being used by some Italian emigrants who sailed on French liners. It was also not unheard of for an Italian to travel to Liverpool and take an English ship, or to Bremen or Hamburg and board a German vessel, though this was the rarer case. Steamship companies were linked to established routes, and Italian emigrants wanting to arrive at a U.S. port not serviced by an Italian line would book passage on the foreign line going to that port. Steamship companies also vied fiercely for the lucrative emigrant business by offering competitive transatlantic fares and on-board accommodations. So Italians seeking a cheaper fare or better accommodations would select a steamship line accordingly. All of this notwithstanding, Italian ports and Italian ships were preferred for sheer convenience.

Prior to 1869 permits to emigrate were issued by regional heads of state, such as the King of the Two Sicilies in Naples or the Duke of Tuscany, through a governmental agency. Since the unification of Italy, passport applications have been made at the local *questura* (police station). *Registri dell'Emigrazione e Passaporti* (Registers of Emigration and Passports) from about 1800 through World War I are preserved in *archivi di stato*, with those dated 1869 and later being among the records of the *Polizia* (Police) or *Prefettura* (Prefect). Passport records since World War I, however, are still in the custody of the *questura* where the application was made. Emigration and passport records usually state the name of each emigrant, *comune* of birth, age or birth date, date when applying to emigrate or date when emigration will be permitted, and the port of departure and destination. Unfortunately, however, in many places, emigration and passport records have not been pre-served, either in the *archivio di stato* or at the *questura*.

A separate set of records dealing with emigration mat-ters has been kept since 1869 by the *Ministero dell'Interno* (Ministry of the Interior) in Rome, where they are main-tained today—closed to public inspection. However, re-quests for genealogical information from these records may be granted if the requestor makes clear his or her relationship to the emigrant and gives a reason for the information that the ministry considers satisfactory.

Archivio Centrale dello Stato (National Archives)

The *Archivio Centrale dello Stato* in Rome is the national repository for the historically valuable records created by the numerous agencies and offices of the Italian govern-ment. These records document the official operations of the government and contain little information of genealogical interest. The *Archivio Centrale*, therefore, is the last civil archives of resort for genealogical research. For specific information about the holdings of the *Archivio Centrale* in Rome, consult the *Guida Generale degli Archivi di Stato Italiani* cited in the bibliography.

2. Religious Record Repositories in Italy

Religious record repositories throughout Italy are as useful to Americans researching their roots as are the civil record respositories described above. Often they are *more* useful, since the registration of baptisms, marriages and burials was initiated by the Catholic Church long before civil authorities assumed responsibility for registering births, marriages and deaths. The vast bulk of religious records in Italy are Roman Catholic. However, records of Jewish and Protestant communities are also available for research. So all three will be discussed in this chapter.

Catholic Records

The Catholic tradition in Italy is ancient, powerful and pervasive. The country is divided into about three hundred *diocesi* (dioceses), which are composed of individual *parrocchie* (parishes). The head of a *diocesi* is a *vescovo* (bishop); the head of a *parrocchia* is a *parroco* (pastor). Every *comune*, regardless of how small it may be, has its own *parrocchia*, and many *comuni* have more than one. In that case, one church is designated the town's *Chiesa Madre* (Mother Church)—sometimes called the *Chiesa Madrice* or, in the north, the *Duomo*. Even a *frazione* may support its own parish. Catholic records are found on both the parochial level and the diocesan level. When corresponding with Roman Catholic parishes in Italy, it may be helpful to consult the *Annuario delle Diocesi d'Italia* (*Annual of the Dioceses of Italy*). This work lists all of the Roman Catholic dioceses of Italy, naming each one's parishes and giving each parish's *comune, provincia* (province) and pastor's name as of 1951. In cities and larger towns with several parishes, finding the right one may entail some trial-and-error searching, for parish boundaries have changed over the years.

Archivi Parrocchiali. Most Catholic Church records of interest to genealogists are still maintained in individual *Archivi Parrocchiali* (Parish Archives). A parish archives consists of the baptismal, marriage and burial registers, and the parish censuses, recorded over the years by the priests. Baptismal, marriage and burial records may be found as early as 1545 (when the Council of Trent first decreed that they be kept), and in a few localities even earlier. However, most parishes will not have any records prior to the early seventeenth century, or even later if the parish was founded later. Catholic Church records are handwritten in a "short-hand" Latin full of abbreviations, or Italian, or—in some areas of the north—local dialect. They survive in every conceivable state of preservation.

Atto di Battesimo. An *Atto di Battesimo* (Baptismal Record) contains: the date the sacrament was administered, name of the priest who presided, name of his parish, date (and sometimes hour) of the infant's birth, name of the father and maiden name of the mother, place of residence of the parents, name given the infant, and the names (and sometimes relationship or place of residence) of two godparents (see illustration on p. 81). When the infant or parents are from another town, the name of that town is given. The entries in many baptismal registers are annotated in the margin with the date and place when the baptized infant married.

Atto di Matrimonio. An *Atto di Matrimonio* (Marriage Record) contains: the date the sacrament was administered,

Page from a typical Catholic baptismal register, recording that the baptism of Emilia Giuseppa Rosa Sorcino (number 11), daughter of Leopoldo and Artamisia Ottaviani, born the previous day, took place on 16 June 1831. Note that Catholic records are in Latin. (*Photograph courtesy of the Latter-day Saints Family History Library.*)

name of the priest who presided, name of the parish, name of the groom and his parents, including his mother's maiden name (sometimes places of residence), name of the bride and her parents, including her mother's maiden name (sometimes places of residence), and the names (and sometimes relationship or places of residence) of two witnesses. When the groom or bride is from another town, the name of that town is given. (Traditionally, a couple is married in the bride's parish. Look there for the record.) When either the groom or bride was married before, the name of the previous spouse is given.

Atto di Sepoltura. An *Atto di Sepoltura* (or *Atto di Seppellimento, Decesso* or *Defunto*) (Burial Record or Death Record) generally contains the date of death, name and age of the deceased person (maiden name when the deceased is a married or widowed woman), and sometimes his or her parents' names (see illustration on p. 83). When the deceased leaves a living spouse, the name of that spouse is given. When the deceased is a widow or widower, the name of the former spouse is given.

About 80 percent of the parish registers of the city of Rome are no longer retained in individual parish archives. They are deposited in the *Archivio Segreto del Vaticano* (Secret Archives of the Vatican), in the *Sezione Archivio del Vicariate di Roma* (Department or Branch of the Vicariate of Rome). Also, the parish registers of the *regione* of Umbria, and those of the *comuni* of Arezzo, Catania, Valdi and Lucerna, are retained in their respective *archivio diocesano* (diocesan archives).

Status Animarum. From around 1700 through the middle of the nineteenth century, Italian parishes used to take a census periodically—sometimes annually, more often at irregular intervals —listing all parishioners by household, sometimes with ages, and indicating their familial relationships. Such a census is called in Latin *Status Animarum*

Page from a typical Catholic burial register, recording that Lorenzo Rossi (number 4) died on 14 February 1812 at the age of about 18 and was buried the following day. (*Photograph courtesy of the Latter-day Saints Family History Library.*)

(State of Souls) or simply *Animae* (Souls); in Italian it is a *Stato delle Anime* or simply *Anime;* and in English it is generally referred to as a Parish Census or Clerical Survey. In parishes where these old clerical surveys have been retained, they may be found among the registers in the *archivio parrocchiale.* They are invaluable for reconstructing eighteenth-century and nineteenth-century families, when it was not unusual for three generations to live under the same roof. They also facilitate interpreting the baptismal, marriage and burial records of the parish. It should be noted, however, that many parishes have not preserved these valuable old parish censuses.

Note that the informational content of baptismal, marriage and burial records, as well as parish censuses, varies a great deal from parish to parish, and that older records generally provide much less information than do the more recent ones. Accuracy, too, varies dramatically in every age.

Archivi Diocesani. Individual dioceses also maintain an archives whose holdings record primarily the official actions of the bishop. These are called either *archivi diocesani* (diocesan archives) or *archivi vescovili* (bishop's archives). Confirmation records (which may also date back to the Council of Trent in 1545) are there since only a bishop may confirm. These registers list the names of people confirmed, dates of their confirmations, and sometimes the names of their sponsors. Records of dispensations granted by the bishop, such as for a marriage between first cousins, show the names of the intended spouses, their residences, the date and nature of the dispensation, and sometimes even a pedigree chart to illustrate the degree of consanguinity. Records of converts to the Catholic Church include the converts' names, residences and ages. There are also records of excommunication, since a bishop may excommunicate from the Church a parishioner of his diocese.

Archivi diocesani often hold the membership records of various Catholic confraternities, institutions and charity organizations, as well as biographical information about the bishops, priests and other Church officials of the diocese. Other registers in an *archivio diocesano* could include records of the administration of the diocese, such as the purchase and sale of Church land, accounts of tenants working and living on Church land, the founding and closing of parishes, and so forth, as well as the *archivi parrocchiali* of defunct parishes. Some registers labelled *Legati* (Legacies) list the names of individuals who willed property to the Church, together with a description of the bequest, or who left funds for annual Masses in remembrance of deceased family members, with the amount. Finally, a diocesan archives often contains a duplicate record of every marriage performed in the diocese, together with baptismal certificates for the bride and groom.

The registers in an *archivio diocesano* may date back to the middle of the sixteenth century and up to the present. The more recent records are still in the custody of the diocesan archives, which may be attached to the bishop's residence or the mother parish of the diocese. But the older registers have sometimes been deposited in *archivi di stato*.

Archivi parrocchiali, *archivi diocesani* and the *Archivio Segreto del Vaticano* are the private archives of the Roman Catholic Church: they are *not* public research institutions. Americans have no moral or legal "right" to the information about their ancestors contained in the old registers of the Church. Access to that information is a privilege.

Access to an *archivio parrocchiale* is a courtesy extended by the pastor of the parish. Americans who have traveled to Italy to trace ancestors in *archivi parrocchiali*, or who have corresponded or tried to correspond with Italian priests, relate vastly different experiences. The reception you receive will vary from one parish to another. Most priests have no staff and are extemely busy not only with their regular liturgical and sacramental duties, but with teaching school, working with youth, organizing community activities, and so forth. Nevertheless, this author's experience

on several research trips to several different parishes has
been that access to *archivi parrocchiali* is usually granted as
long as the researcher uses them during the hours when the
sacristy is normally open, and does not expect assistance
from the priest. Parish priests are seldom trained historians
or archivists. On the contrary, it is becoming increasingly
common to encounter Church officials who can neither
decipher nor translate the Latin script that fills the ancient
ecclesiastical registers. On only one occasion did this
author fail to gain access to a parish archives, and that was
due more to logistical problems with the pastor than to any
set policy. Not all Americans, though, have had a similarly
happy research experience.

Showing respect and deference when dealing with
religious authorities in Italy is not only diplomatically
expedient, but appropriate to the culture (for more on the
importance of writing letters of introduction and understanding the cultural context, see the Postscript at the end
of this guide). In addition, since access to a parish archives
is a favor, it is common courtesy for a researcher to return
the favor with equal kindness. Showing your appreciation
by leaving a generous gift "for the needs of the church"—
candles or flowers for the altar, a donation toward the
restoration of the organ, a series of Masses for your ancestors—is a proper and deeply appreciated gesture. This
author has never been charged a fee for a church record.
On the other hand, an Italian priest would be delinquent
in his responsibilities if he did not remind the American
genealogist gaining information from his records that his
parish has many needs and can always use a new source
of revenue.

Access to an *archivio diocesano* is gained from the designated person on the bishop's staff. It is generally granted
if, once again, the researcher displays proper attitude and
decorum, ability and seriousness, flexibility and appreciation, and uses the archives during the hours when the

episcopal office is normally open—and without constant assistance from the bishop's staff. Access to the *Archivio Segreto del Vaticano* is obtained from the appropriate official on the Pope's staff and is generally granted only to university professors and published scholars.

If you are unable to find the religious records you need, ask for the name and address of the local church historian or antiquary. This is the person—official or unofficial—who is most familiar with the whereabouts of the church records created in his or her province or region. Contact this person and ask for assistance.

Jewish Records

Jewish resources have survived that warrant mention, for they pre-date the Italian civil records already discussed in chapter 1, and are therefore invaluable to Americans tracing Jewish ancestors who were Italian. Jewish communities have existed throughout the Italian peninsula and Sicily since the time of the Roman Republic, making Italian Jewry the oldest in Europe. From antiquity through the Middle Ages Italian Jews were concentrated in the city of Rome and the Kingdom of the Two Sicilies, with few living in the north. Italy was a meeting place of Jewish exiles from many countries of the West and East, and their mingling engendered an extraordinarily vibrant culture.

In the thirteenth century the Jews of Italy began migrating northward. This migration accelerated in 1492 when the Spanish monarchs of the Kingdom of the Two Sicilies (King Ferdinand and Queen Isabella) expelled from their realm all Jews who refused to convert to Christianity. The Spanish Inquisition caused many southern Jews to move up to the Papal States (Rome still has the largest Jewish population in Italy) and major northern cities such as Turin, Milan, Genoa, Florence and Venice. It was in these prosperous urban centers that Italian Jewish civilization enjoyed its "Golden Age" during the Renaissance. But

Jewish "ghettos" developed in many of the smaller towns and villages of the north as well.

The word "ghetto" is itself of northern Italian origin. Although its precise etymology is "hotly debated by historians and linguists," writes Riccardo Calimani in *The Ghetto of Venice* (see bibliography), "the commonly accepted opinion is that *ghetto* is a Venetian word denoting an enclosed area where the Jews were obliged to live. In earlier times, the site occupied by the ghetto was the site of a foundry, called *geto* in Venetian dialect. . . ." Many illustrious rabbinic families derive from this "Golden Age" of Italian Jewish culture. The Abravanel family, for instance, traces its proud history back to Venice, and the famous Luria family is believed to have taken its name from the northern Italian village of Loria.

The Jewish population of Italy peaked in the seventeenth century at about 50,000. Since then it has declined steadily. Most of Italy's Jewish communities had disappeared by the close of World War II, and the Jewish population of Italy today stands at about 35,000. One of the many destinations of emigrating Italian Jews has been the United States, and the descendants of these immigrants have a variety of resources to utilize to trace their ancestry.

Jewish Local History. Prior to seeking original records, you should know the *comune* where your ancestors lived and learn as much as possible from published materials about that *comune*'s Jews. A good place to start if you do not know the native town of your family is Samuele Schaert's *I Cognomi degli Ebrei d'Italia* (*Surnames of the Jews of Italy*). This book indicates the place of origin of many Italian Jewish surnames. Once you know your ancestral *comune*, consult Annie Sacerdoti's *Guida all'Italia Ebraica* (*Guide to Jewish Italy*), which surveys, region by region, *comune* by *comune*, all of Italy's Jewish communities—those defunct and those still thriving. Sacerdoti provides a brief historical sketch of each community, followed by a description of its synagogue, cemeteries, and any museums, libraries or research centers devoted to Jewish history and culture in the *comune*. (An English translation of this work exists (see bibliography); however, its historical sketches are not as detailed as those of the original Italian edition.)

There is an extensive corpus of Italian "Jewish local history." For a bibliographic listing of recent works dealing with the history of the Jews in Italy, including works about particular localities and families, consult Aldo Luzzatto's *Biblioteca Italo-Ebraica* (*The Italo-Jewish Library*). Substantial histories of individual Jewish communities, such as Riccardo Calimani's *The Ghetto of Venice* (cited above), or Shlomo Simonsohn's *History of the Jews of the Duchy of Mantua*, for example, are often published in English. They usually contain a lengthy bibliography of related works which direct you to additional secondary literature as well as documentary sources valuable for your family research. They are also indexed by personal name, and some, such as Simonsohn's, by place names and subjects, too!

Published Genealogies. To exploit the resources available in American libraries, you should also try to discover whether a genealogy of your family has already appeared in print. Nello Pavoncello has begun a series of books titled *Antiche Famiglie Ebraiche Italiane* (*Ancient Italian Jewish Families*). Volume I, published in 1982, contains the histories of twenty families reprinted from articles appearing between 1957 and 1960 in the *Settimanale Israel* (*Israel Weekly*). But no subsequent volume has yet appeared.

Sometimes the genealogy of a Jewish family will appear as part of a larger work. For example, in Vittore Colorni's *Judaica Minora: Saggi sulla Storia dell'Ebraismo Italiano dall'-Antichita all'Età Moderna* (*Judaica Minora: Essays on the History of Italian Judaism from Antiquity to Modern Times*) (Milan: Dott. A. Giuffre, Editore, 1983) there are two essays which trace two prominent Jewish families—Finzi and Colorni—generation by generation, from the fifteenth century to the present day. Less detailed Jewish family histories appear in "Parnassim: Le Grande Famiglie Ebraiche Italiane dal Secolo XI al XIX" ("Parnassim: The Great Italian Jewish Families from the Eleventh to the Nineteenth Century"), by Franco Pisa. This series of articles appeared from 1980 through 1984 in the *Annuario di Studi Ebraici* (*Annual of Jewish Studies*), edited by Ariel Toaff.

Journals. Another way to prepare to search for Jewish forefathers in Italian records is to read pertinent journals. Three genealogical quarterlies—two specifically Jewish, one specifically Italian—have recently included articles about researching Jewish ancestors in Italy. They will likely be printing more such articles in the future.

"Italian Research," by Marsha Saron Dennis, appeared in *Dorot*, the newsletter of the Jewish Genealogical Society, Inc., in the Autumn 1989 issue. Based on her own experience, Dennis offers advice on what to do, and what *not* to do, to insure success in your research trip to Italy.

"The Ghetto of Verona," by Mark Tedeschi, appeared in *AVOTAYNU, the International Review of Jewish Genealogy* in the Fall 1988 issue. His article provides research information and advice based on his own experience tracing ancestors in Verona.

POINTers, the quarterly journal of POINT (Pursuing Our Italian Names Together), published an article by Dale Leppart in the Summer 1991 issue. In "Researching a Judaic Family in Italy" Leppart relates his surprise at discovering Jewish ancestors in his Italian family tree. From the time of the Spanish Inquisition to the present day, generation to generation, the family had guarded the secret of their Jewishness.

The quarterly titled *SEARCH*, published by the Jewish Genealogical Society of Illinois, may also contain a piece on Italian Jewry from time to time.

Writing the Rabbi. After you have learned the *comune* of your ancestors, send a letter to the rabbi there. If none of the resources cited above gives you the rabbi's name and address, consult *The Jewish Travel Guide* published annually by Jewish Chronicle Publications (25 Furnival St., London EC4A 1JT, England). It lists all extant organized Jewish communities around the world and provides addresses. The rabbi of your ancestors' *comune* will be able to inform you as to the extent and location of the surviving records for his community. If your ancestors' community has disappeared, as most of the smaller ones have, write to the rabbi of the closest synagogue still existing.

Records of birth, marriage and death have survived for many Jewish communities, and may date back as far as the seventeenth century. These are usually kept in the local synagogue, but *may* be part of the *archivio comunale* (see below). The rabbi will also know whether there is a Jewish museum, library or research center in your ancestor's *comune*. You will want to send a letter there as well.

Civil Repositories. It is often possible to find a miscellaneous assortment of records relating specifically to the Jews of a particular *comune* in the *archivio comunale*, as well as in the *archivio di stato* serving the *comune*'s province. Such records may include registrations of births, marriages and deaths. Some notarial records dating back to the fourteenth century (sometimes even earlier) deal with the legal transactions, court cases, inheritance disputes, and other matters involving individual Jews. In *The Jews of the Duchy of Milan*, four volumes published in 1986, Shlomo Simonsohn has printed—in English translation, with notes and text in English—all of the Jewish notarial records for the area around Milan from the Middle Ages through the sixteenth century. Sometimes substantial documentation on rabbinical families is also found in *archivi comunali* and *archivi di stato*. Special census enumerations were often made of the inhabitants of Jewish ghettos, too. In the *Archivio di Stato* in Verona, for example, is a manuscript book from 1776 which contains a detailed description of the Jewish ghetto of that city. It includes a map of the ghetto and a house-by-house census listing not only the occupants' names, but also their occupations.

Catholic Repositories. Since a large portion of Italy's Jewish population has lived for centuries—especially since 1492—in the area that comprised the Papal States, various records pertaining to Jews can also be found in the *Archivio Segreto del Vaticano*. *Catasti* are one of these. Unfortunately, access to Vatican archives is not easily secured.

University Records. At times in history Jews have occupied influential and much-respected positions in the universities of Italy. Therefore, *registri delle università* (university registers) may also prove valuable to Jewish genealogy (see chapter 3).

Cemeteries. A trip to your ancestor's *comune* will allow you to exploit a resource not in American libraries and not available through correspondence (unless you have a researcher in Italy): cemeteries. Jewish cemeteries in Italy are unlike Christian cemeteries (see Postscript) insofar as the individual graves, with their individual headstones, are maintained in perpetuity. So you may be able to use names and dates inscribed on cemetery monuments to extend your family tree. In some instances, however, monuments dating back to the seventeenth century and earlier bear only the name of the deceased, and no date of birth or death. And, of course, some of the older cemeteries were destroyed years ago. Many, however, are still maintained.

Patronymics. Jews of Italy did not commonly use surnames prior to the seventeenth century. Knowing the given names of your ancestors becomes vital for research prior to that time, therefore, because only their given names and patronymics will identify them. Knowing your ancestor's *comune* of birth also becomes especially critical for research prior to the general adoption of surnames among Jews, since only the particular place name following your ancestor's given name and patronymic will distinguish him or her from others with an identical name and patronymic.

Centers for Jewish Studies. Finally, Americans seeking Jewish ancestors who were Italian should not overlook the collections housed in two major centers for Jewish studies. At the Diaspora Research Institute (Tel Aviv University, Ramat Aviv, Tel Aviv 69978, Israel) Professor Shlomo Simonsohn is devoting himself to publishing a complete documentary history of the Jews in Italy. His books of Milan's notarial records (cited above) constitute part of that project. The Centro di Studi sull'Ebraismo Italiano (27 Hillel Street, Jerusalem, Israel), under the direction of Miriam Della Pergola, holds 6,000 books on Italian Jewry and many journals with articles on the Jewish communities of Italy.

In 1492 when so many Italian Jews migrated north of Naples because of the Spanish Inquisition, many others emigrated to other lands. In subsequent centuries many of these same families, experiencing persecution or facing expulsion by royal decree, removed yet again to the United States. Consequently, American Jews may trace their ancestors back to Italy via some intermediate country, and then discover that their ancestors originally migrated into the Italian peninsula or Sicily from any one of numerous *other* countries of both West and East. So your "Italianità" ("Italian-ness") may turn out to be only one chapter in the larger tome of your Jewish heritage. Your searching is not over yet!

Protestant Records

The number of Protestants in Italy has always been small—smaller certainly than the number of Jews—and the

Protestant population has historically been concentrated in an area in the Alps called the Waldensian Valleys. However, although Protestants have made up only a tiny fraction of the total Italian population, the majority of Italian immigrants to the United States prior to 1820 were Waldenses. For the descendants of these early immigrants who are researching their Protestant Italian roots, therefore, a description of the most important resources to consult is in order.

Waldenses. The Waldenses were followers of Peter Waldo, a twelfth-century separatist whose teachings were essentially "Protestant" three centuries before the Reformation. The majority of Waldenses lived in several inaccessible valleys in the Alps in the *regione* of *Piemonte* (Piedmont), about thirty miles southwest of *Torino* (Turin)—an area that flip-flopped many times over the centuries between French and Italian domination. So they managed to remain a cohesive and isolated religious sect out of the disciplinary reach of the Roman Church until the sixteenth century, when the Waldenses aligned with the Protestant Reformation. A century of persecution and religious wars followed that failed to eliminate the Waldenses, and freedom of worship was finally granted to them by law in 1848. In 1900 the Waldensian Valleys, the Pinerolo District, and the city of Turin, contained a population of perhaps 22,500 Waldenses divided into seventeen parishes. That same year, 1900, the total number of Protestants in Italy—resulting from the missionary efforts of Baptist, Methodist, Seventh-Day Adventist and other Protestant ministers who started arriving in the 1860s—was around 33,000. To this day Waldenses (perhaps 25,000 to 35,000 strong) remain the vast majority of Protestants in Italy. Recently they united with the Baptists and Methodists to form the *Chiesa Evangelica Italiana* (Italian Evangelical Church) with headquarters in Rome.

Page from a marriage register of a Waldensian parish in the *comune* of Torre Pellice, *provincia* of Torino, recording that on April 9, 1750, Jean Bonjour, son of Daniel (deceased), married Marie Baridon, daughter of Daniel (deceased) and widow of Philippe Garoupin, Sr. Note that the records are in French and the names are French, reflecting the fact that this area in the Alps was at times under French dominion. Note, too, the use of the Italian term *"fu."* (*Photograph courtesy of the Latter-day Saints Family History Library.*)

Records of the Protestant parishes of Italy are similar in content to those of the Catholic parishes, and they are also still in the custody of the individual parishes (see illustration on p. 95). The LDS FHL has microfilmed the registers of sixteen Waldensian parishes in the Pinerolo District. These contain entries from about 1685 to the present day. The registers of eight other Waldensian parishes that could not be filmed are currently being transcribed by hand. Also available from the LDS FHL are forty-three rolls of microfilm that constitute what is called the "Piedmont Project." These rolls contain hundreds of family group sheets compiled from the microfilmed parish registers, as well as an alphabetical surname index to them.

It is noteworthy that the *archivio di stato* in Turin has Waldensian notarial records beginning in 1610. For their possible genealogical value, see the description of *Minute, Atti e Bastardelli Notarili* in chapter 1.

Non-Italian Protestants. Many of Italy's Protestant parishes were founded and are maintained for the benefit of foreign residents—diplomats, business people, writers, artists, and so forth. Revalee Stevens, herself an American residing in Italy, has begun a series of books transcribing records pertaining to Protestant Americans in Italy. *North American Records in Italy: The Protestant Cemetery of Rome* (Baton Rouge, La.: Oracle Press, 1981) contains the burial records and monument transcriptions of all Americans interred in Rome's Protestant Cemetery. *Protestant Records in Italy: The Registers of St. Paul's Within-the-Walls* (Baton Rouge, La.: Oracle Press, 1985) contains the baptismal, marriage and burial records of American citizens in the registers of Rome's largest Protestant church.

Whether your Italian ancestors turn out to be Catholic, Jewish or Protestant, therefore, a plentiful variety of religious resource materials, both primary and secondary, are available to help you climb your family tree.

3. Libraries and Other Resources in Italy

Besides civil and religious archives, Italy has other repositories of resource materials useful to Americans pursuing Italian genealogical research. These include, most importantly, Italy's *biblioteche* (libraries). But several other kinds of specialized collections will also be described in this chapter.

Biblioteche

Italy has a well-organized national library system. There is no single "national library" analogous to the Bibliothèque Nationale in Paris or the Library of Congress in Washington. Rome, Florence, Bari, Milan, Naples, Palermo, Turin and Venice all have a *Biblioteca Nazionale* (national library). Each one is named for an illustrious Italian —such as the *Biblioteca Nazionale Vittorio Emanuele III* in Naples—and collects and preserves published and primary materials relating to its own area within Italy. All house not only published volumes, but many manuscript collections of personal and family papers donated or bequeathed by local families, too. The libraries of Rome and Florence, with the elevated status of "Central National Libraries," serve also as depository libraries for all printed matter published in Italy, as well as foreign works pertinent to Italian civilization.

There are, however, smaller libraries in other provincial capitals, as well as *biblioteche comunali* (local libraries) in many *comuni*, which hold materials on local history and genealogy, too. Italy's university libraries also fall within the national library system. They are located in Bologna, Cagliari, Catania, Genoa, Messina, Modena, Naples, Padua, Pavia, Pisa, Rome and Sassari and are meant to support the research and study needs of the faculty and students of Italy's universities.

Francesco Marraro's *Repertorio delle Biblioteche Italiane* (*Repertory of Italian Libraries*) is a complete listing by region, and thereunder by province, of all of Italy's libraries. It includes the address and hours of each library, as well as the number of volumes and periodicals each one holds. Before approaching the *biblioteca nazionale* serving your ancestor's area, therefore, you can locate and consult a smaller, local library. *The Guide to Italian Libraries and Archives*, compiled by Rudolf J. Lewanski and intended specifically for American researchers, offers practical information about Italy's libraries and archives, as well as an overview of the entire national system. This work is invaluable as all of Italy's libraries have their own rules and regulations governing admission, hours of operation, photocopying and so forth. Lewanski provides all of this useful information.

Archivi Genealogici

Genealogical Archives are collections of published and original materials pertaining to royal and noble families and to the clergy. These may be found as a separate collection or department in Italy's ninety-five *archivi di stato*, or in any one of the eight *biblioteche nazionale*, or sometimes even in *biblioteche comunali* and university libraries. *Archivi genealogici* contain heraldic, ecclesiastical and genealogical materials, sometimes dating back to the twelfth century. The head of a noble family was literally the ruler of his estates, on which there were towns and villages. The noble was law-maker and judge to the men, women and children who populated his towns and villages and worked his land. So *archivi genealogici* include the acts and judgments of the heads of titled families regarding all kinds of political, judicial and administrative matters, as well as pedigree charts and coats-of-arms.

Americans who trace their ancestry back to a titled family of Italy will find their family histories already published and available in the libraries of Italy. These published genealogies have already been described in the Introduction. Rarely, however, do *archivi genealogici* contain anything of family history value to descendants of Italy's *popolino*.

Archivi Ecclesiastici

Ecclesiastical Archives are collections of materials regarding the clergy of the Church. They include a variety of documents dating back to the thirteenth century that detail the names of members of the clergy, sometimes with birth dates and birthplaces, and family relationships. *Archivi ecclesiastici* may be found in *archivi di stato*, the *Archivio Segreto del Vaticano*, and sometimes *archivi diocesani*.

Registri delle Università

If an ancestor of yours was a scholar, you may wish to consult the *Registri dell'Università* (University Registers) where he or she studied or taught. Such registers may be found either in *archivi di stato* or at the university, and they may date back to the thirteenth century, as do those of Padua and Bologna, two of the oldest universities in the world. They are generally kept by school, so you must know whether your ancestor was in medicine, law, theology, history, philosophy, and so forth. Student records are indexed by surname for each freshman class. After locating your ancestor in the index, you may consult his or her admission record, which provides the freshman's name, birth date and birthplace, as well as his or her father's name and occupation.

When you are certain, based on this information, that you are dealing with the right student, proceed to consult his or her academic file. It will provide complete information about his or her scholarly activities at the university. There are also registers with information about instructors. The genealogical boon of *registri dell'università* is that often, when you find one ancestor, you discover other family members there, too, sometimes for succeeding generations.

Genealogical Institutions in Italy

Given the Italians' lack of interest in genealogy *per se*, but their keen interest in heraldry, genealogical institutions in Italy —like the *archivi genealogici* discussed above—tend to focus on ancient noble and royal lineages, and not on the *popolino*. The largest genealogical institution in Italy is the *Istituto Genealogico Italiano* (Italian Genealogical Institute) (Via Torta 14, 50122 Firenze), which was founded in 1877 as the *Ufficio Araldico Italiano* (Italian Heraldic Office). An on-going project of this institution is the preparation of a general index to all manuscripts in Italy dealing with genealogy and heraldry. To date the index includes about four million surnames and 200,000 coats-of-arms. You can write the director of the *Istituto Genealogico Italiano* for specific information about his collections. He will not conduct research for you, but will let you know if your family's surname appears in the index.

The Italian Genealogical & Heraldic Institute (Via Massimo d'Azeglio, 9-B, 90143 Palermo), under the direction of Cav. Louis Mendola, a distinguished heraldist, is another private institution that may be of help in tracing titled families of Italy.

Finally, Trafford R. Cole, Ph.D., an American who has lived and worked in Italy for twenty years, runs another "Italian Genealogical Institute" (Via Modigliani, 1B, 35020 Albignasego (PD)). Cole is an Accredited Genealogist and author of numerous works in English on Italian genealogy (see bibliography).

Postscript:
Practical Suggestions for
Exploiting Italian Records

Finding and using the Italian records that pertain to your family may take considerable time and effort. So you want to reap the greatest informational harvest from your research labors. Here are a few suggestions that will help you use Italian records to the fullest. Heeding these observations will not only facilitate your research, but will result in a family history that is rich in *Italianità* as well.

Write Letters of Introduction

The value of writing letters of introduction, and good, concise business letters in general, cannot be over-emphasized. First of all, let the archivist, or the pastor of the parish, or the clerk in the town hall, know who you are and what records you expect to find and use in his repository. Ask the days and hours of operation, too. These letters are appreciated by Italian officials, who would rather *you* do the research than ask *them* to do it. The responses you receive will either confirm or correct your expectations and help you schedule your time and activities. If you take them with you, the replies also serve as handy "door openers" when you arrive at the institution.

English is not spoken by every Italian, as you may have heard. Many priests, clerks, archivists and librarians *can*

103

get by in English. Usually, though, they remember only a few words and expressions from school days, and have trouble providing clear information or instruction in English. The best policy is to write in Italian. Sample letters in Italian addressed to both civil and religious archives, with English translations, may be found in the works of Cole and Konrad (see bibliography) and in *POINTers*, Vol. 5, No. 4, Winter 1991. You may find assistance in drafting letters in Italian and translating replies from an elderly relative, neighbor, local librarian or Italian teacher, or from fellow members of a genealogical society. Use an English-Italian dictionary to familiarize yourself with a few key phrases of politeness, and learn the terms for the records you will be seeking. The glossary at the end of this chapter is intended to help you with this. And by all means, keep the dictionary with you on your research trip to Italy. If, however, you have no choice but to write in English, compose short, simple sentences, and be as brief and precise as possible. You may receive a reply in Italian, broken English, English . . . or no reply at all.

Whether you write in Italian or English, though, when requesting civil records be sure to ask for the *atto integrale* (complete record); otherwise the official will send a short-form certificate that does not include parents' names and possibly other information contained in the original.

Always enclose a couple of international postal reply coupons with your letters. When writing to civil archives, as a courtesy, offer to pay whatever fee may be charged for the service. When writing to a priest, enclose an offering "for the church" (as already discussed in chapter 2 under *Archivi Parrocchiali*).

Never send cash, of course; it is easy to obtain a draft check in lire (or any other foreign currency). Simply call Thomas Cook Currency Services, Inc., at 1-800-368-5683. A draft check in the amount you specify, made payable to whomever you specify, is mailed to you. Payment—including a service fee of ten dollars—may be made by MasterCard or Visa, or personal check.

Prepare Materials for Communication

When visiting the towns of your ancestors, as valuable as mastering a basic vocabulary of Italian words is taking along a family tree chart . . . which is worth a thousand words. The chart should be simple and basic, showing direct lines of descent only. Displaying the chart to the villagers strolling in the *piazza* (town square), waiting at the bus stop, or gossiping in the market, as well as to the officials of the repositories you will be using, will make clear what you are doing and what you need. The villagers, if only to satisfy their curiosity, will pay attention and offer direction.

Know the Cultural Context

Being able to translate into English the words found in an Italian record is not always sufficient to understanding the full informational content of that record. It is often helpful, and sometimes necessary, to be familiar with the cultural context in which the record was created. Here are four examples that demonstrate the importance of being familiar with the cultural context for understanding Italian records:

Interpreting Italian Terms. Because of numerous and distinct dialects, the same term may take on different meanings in different parts of Italy, or in records of different centuries. Records created in mountainous terrain may contain terms peculiar to occupations of that setting, such as viniculture or mining, while records created in coastal towns may contain words peculiar to seafaring activities. Even a term as deceptively simple as *fattoria* or *podere*, translated in Italian-English dictionaries as "farm,"

can mislead American researchers who do not know what constitutes a farm in Italy. Americans might picture farms as they exist in New England or the Midwest, with neighboring families separated by miles of fields or pastures. In Italy, farmers reside together in the town or village, with neighbors of all other trades and professions, in streets lined with adjoining houses. The fields they tend surround the town or village. Up until the twentieth century, small livestock could be kept at home, in the courtyard or ground level of the farmer's house. Large herds and flocks remained on the farm land beyond the town limits.

In a society as rigidly divided into classes as Italy has traditionally been over the centuries, the use of titles may vary in meaning and significance in different places and times, too. *Maestro*, for example, meaning "Master" (*Magister* in Latin), is often found in old Italian records before the name of a craftsman. This term of respect would indicate that the craftsman had achieved a level of mastery which entitled him to take on apprentices—and use the title. The term *Don* before a man's name, and *Donna* before a woman's name, may or may not indicate noble birth. For they were used not only for persons of noble rank, but for persons whose families were of noble origin, but reduced in circumstances as well. Such "downward mobility" occurred often and everywhere, for a variety of reasons, throughout Italy's nobility. Often, too, *don* and *donna* were simply titles of respect and deference used for a man or woman of some standing in the community—wealth, or education, or position—achieved *not* through inheritance, but rather through self-improvement.

Italian Cemeteries. In Italy some wealthy families own mausoleums in perpetuity. Since mausoleums hold a limited number of caskets, as family members die, the older caskets are removed to make room for the new. The bones from the removed casket are dropped into the ossuary beneath the mausoleum. A marble plaque on the door or wall of the mausoleum is inscribed with the names and death dates of those who have been buried in the mausoleum.

The vast majority of Italian families, however, do not own mausoleums. For their deceased members they lease graves for twenty or thirty years. At the end of that time, if the lease is not renewed, the casket is removed from the grave and the bones are placed in the large ossuary serving the entire cemetery.

Americans of Italian descent, therefore—unless their family was titled or just rich and owned a mausoleum—should not expect to discover the graves of their nineteenth-century or earlier ancestors in the cemetery of the family's native town in Italy. Those graves will have changed occupants many times over the years!

It is also customary in Italy to adorn cemetery monuments with a portrait photograph of the deceased person. As you walk down the paths of an Italian cemetery, therefore, the departed stare at you.

Naming Tradition. Since at least the sixteenth century, on the mainland of Italy as well as the islands of Sicily and Sardinia, tradition has dictated how Italian parents name their children. A couple's first son is given the name of the father's father; the first daughter is given the name of the father's mother. The second son is given the name of the mother's father; the second daughter is given the name of the mother's mother. Subsequent children are usually given their parents' names or the names of favorite or unmarried or deceased aunts and uncles. Exceptions do exist. The father's father might suggest, for example, that the grandson about to be given his name be baptized instead in the name of a son of his who died in infancy or childhood many years earlier. This is especially common when no other member of the family bears the name of that deceased son. Such a wish would be honored, and a subsequent son would be named for the father's father. Or the mother's mother may ask that the daughter to be named after her be given the name of a particular saint to whom she holds a special devotion. This would be done, and a subsequent daughter would be named for the mother's mother. Though the tradition cannot be assumed to have been followed in every case, it does provide plausible leads to pursue regarding parents' names.

Fu. Literally, *fu* means "was." In Italian records it is used to indicate a deceased person. When the father or mother of an individual named in a record is still living at the time the record is created, the relationship is indicated using *di*. For example, "Ignazio, figlio di Francesco" means "Ignazio, son of Francesco, who is living." However, when the parent is deceased at the time the record is created, the relationship is indicated using *del fu* for the father or *della fu* for the mother. For example, "Ignazio, figlio del fu Francesco" means "Ignazio, son of the deceased Frances-co." "Giovanni, figlio della fu Rosalia" means "Giovanni, son of the deceased Rosalia." But frequently, for exped-ience, the *del* or *della* would be dropped, and the word *fu* was simply used in place of the word *di* to indicate a deceased parent; for example, "Concetta, figlia fu An-tonio." This practice may be helpful when searching for an ancestor's date of death. For example, if an 1842 marriage record indicates the mother of the bride Giuseppa as "di Maria," and the 1844 marriage record of Giuseppa's sister Anna gives her mother as "fu Maria," it is evident that Maria died sometime between the marriage dates of her daughters Giuseppa and Anna in 1842 and 1844.

In short, for Americans to reap the greatest harvest from their examination of Italian records, they should famil-iarize themselves with the history of the people, the place and the time where those records were originally created. This may be done by seeking out and reading works of local history, the books about the particular *comune, provincia* or *regione* where your family lived in Italy, as discussed in the Introduction to this guide. Another way to learn local customs and language is to familiarize yourself as much as possible with the oral history of your ancestors' *paese*.

Local Oral History

When you begin to correspond with relatives in Italy, or with a hired professional genealogist, or when you visit your ancestral town yourself, be sure to inquire about local oral history. Every area of Italy is still rich in oral history that only people in the local area can relate to you from memory. You will not find it in books, because it is not written down. Or if someone *has* committed it to writing, you will find it probably as a fascicle of typescript or manuscript pages in a parish archives or local library. Often it was the pastor of a rural parish—a man of some education and an intellectual penchant with no other way to exercise it—who took an interest in the history of his community. He may have simply organized the parish archives, or examined his own and other local records for information about the origin of his community, and then assembled that information in writing.

One example of this is *Il Prezioso* (*The Precious Book*) found in the *biblioteca comunale* of Erice, a town near Trapani, Sicily. In the late seventeenth century the town's *parroco*, Don Vito Carvini, penned this manuscript in Latin on a thousand folios of vellum. *Il Prezioso* tells part of the story of the *comune* of Erice as derived from original sixteenth- and seventeenth-century notarial and parish records—some of which no longer exist—and contains a wealth of genealogical information about some of Erice's early families. For instance, six generations of the Giannitrapani family can be established by combining the information from several entries in the text of *Il Prezioso*. In the villages of your ancestors, therefore, await sources you could never have known existed, could never have found outside the *comune*. Always bear in mind, though, that secondary sources such as these are liable to contain errors. It is best to verify their content against the original records.

Plan Your Transportation and Lodging

Plan your transportation and lodging as thoroughly as you can before crossing the Atlantic. Most places in Italy are easily accessible by rail or bus, or on foot; but for some, you must rent a car. Learning the transportation situation in the region where your ancestors lived will save you a great deal of time and aggravation. Also, not every *comune* has a hotel or *pensione*. Italian government tourist offices in major U.S. cities, such as New York, Chicago and San Francisco, can often furnish more detailed and more pertinent information for your trip to Italy than can U.S. travel agents. Italian Tourist Offices usually have the names and addresses of all categories of lodgings from four or five stars down to *pensioni* listed by province or region. (The government sets the price for each category.) They can also supply transportation and restaurant information for the cities or major towns you expect to visit, as well as superb road maps. A letter to the *sindaco* in the *municipio* can also clarify these matters . . . and prepare your way.

Closing

In Italy there is little interest in genealogy. Italians do not have to search to learn who their grandparents were, where they lived, and how they lived, or their great-grandparents, either. They already know. Every day they live their cultural history. For Italians have tended—until the twentieth century—to remain for generations in the *comune* of their birth, the *comune* of their ancestors. This is due to the strong attachment to their *famiglia* and the profound love of their *paese*, for which Italians are justly famed.

In the United States, however, Americans of Italian descent, cut off two or three generations ago from their families' roots, must engage in research to rediscover those roots. Understandably, Italian Americans in ever increasing numbers are taking up genealogy. It requires learning new information and mastering new skills; it calls for determination and patience, too. But once you have found your family's *comune* in Italy, you can often trace your ancestors back two, three or more centuries, perhaps even—if you are particularly dedicated and particularly lucky—to the late Middle Ages, because your Italian ancestors were people attached to their beloved *paese*. And it is precisely their attachment to their beloved *paese* that makes their voyage to America the most astounding and poignant chapter in Italian-American family history.

Glossary

This glossary contains all Italian words used in this guide, as well as a selection of other Italian nouns an American is likely to encounter when searching in Italian records. Plural endings are given in parentheses. Adjectival forms are not given since they are easily recognizable from the noun forms.

Famiglia (Famiglie) = Family (Families)

antenato(i) = ancestor(s)
bambina(e) = child(ren) (fem.)
bambino(i) = child(ren) (masc.)
bisnonna(e) = great-grandmother(s)
bisnonno(i) = great-grandfather(s)
capostipite = founder of the family; earliest ancestor
cognome(i) = surname(s)
cugina(e) = cousin(s) (fem.)
cugino(i) = cousin(s) (masc.)
don = title of respect for a man
donna = title of respect for a woman
famiglia(e) nobile(i) = noble family(ies)
famiglia(e) notabile(i) = noteworthy family(ies)
famiglia(e) estinte(i) = extinct family(ies)
famiglia(e) fiorente(i) = flourishing family(ies)
femmina(e) = female(s)
fratello(i) = brother(s)
genitora(e) = mother(s)
genitore(i) = father(s) or parent(s)
genitori ignoti = parents unknown

madre(-) = mother(s)
madre ignota = mother unknown
maestro(i) = master(s)
maschio(-) = male(s)
nobilità = nobility
nobiliario(-) = book(s) of nobility
nome(i) = name(s)
nonna(e) = grandmother(s)
nonno(i) = grandfather(s)
padre(i) = father(s)
padre ignoto = father unknown
padrina(e) = godmother(s)
padrino(i) = godfather(s)
parente(i) = relative(s)
persona(e) = person(s)
sorella(e) = sister(s)
zia(e) = aunt(s)
zio(i) = uncle(s)

Stato (Stati) = State (States)

campagna = countryside or unimproved land
città(e) = city(ies)
cittadina(e) = citizen(s) (fem.)
cittadino(i) = citizen(s) (masc.)
comune(i) = township(s)
contadina(e) or paesana(e) = peasant(s) (fem.)
contadino(i) or paesano(i) = peasant(s) (masc.)
distretto(i) = district(s)
frazione(i) = village(s) or hamlet(s)
Italia = Italy
Italianità = "Italian-ness"
ministero(i) = ministry(ies)
municipio(-) = town hall(s)
paese(i) = town(s) or countryside
patria(e) = country(ies)
polizia = police
popolino = common people
popolo = people or population
prefetto(i) = prefect(s)
prefettura(e) = prefecture(s)
provincia(e) = province(s)

questura(e) = police station(s)
re(-) = king(s)
regione(i) = region(s)
sindaco(hi) = mayor(s)
ufficio(-) = office(s)

Archivio(-) = Archives

annuario(-) = annual(s) or yearbook(s)
araldica = heraldry
atto(i) = record(s) or deed(s)
bastardelli = type of index for notarial records
beni immobili = real estate
beni mobili = personal estate
bibliografia(e) = bibliography(ies)
biblioteca(he) = library(ies)
biografia(e) = biography(ies)
blasone(i) = coat(s)-of-arms
catalogo(hi) = catalogue(s)
catasto(i) = tax assessment(s) or tax list(s)
censimento(i) or censo(i) = census(es)
certificato(i) = certificate(s)
cimitero(i) = cemetery(ies)
dizionario(-) = dictionary(ies)
documento(i) = document(s)
emigrazione = emigration
enciclopedia(e) = encyclopedia(e)
fu = was (deceased)
genealogia(e) = genealogy(ies)
giornale(i) = newspaper(s)
guida(e) = guide(s)
immobiliare = real estate
leva = conscription or draft
libro(i) = book(s)
minuta(e) = rough draft(s)
morto(i) = dead person(s)
nascita(e) = birth(s)
notaio (notai) = notary (notaries)
passaporto(i) = passport(s)
promessa(e) = promise(s)
registro(i) = register(s)

residenza(e) = residence(s)
ricerca(che) = research
riveli = tax declarations
sezione(i) = department(s) or branch(es)
stato civile = vital records
stemma(e) = coat(s)-of-arms
storia(e) = history
ufficiale di anagrafe = official of the census
ufficiale di stato civile = official of vital records
ufficio di anagrafe or ufficio anagrafico = office of the census
ufficio di stato civile = office of vital records

Chiesa (Chiese) = Church (Churches)

anima(e) = soul(s)
arciprete(i) = head priest
battesimo(i) = baptism(s)
Chiesa Cattolica = Catholic Church
cresima(e) = confirmation(s)
decesso(i) = deceased person(s)
defunto(i) = deceased person(s)
diocesi(-) = diocese(s)
legati = legacies
matrimonio(-) = marriage(s)
parrocchia(e) = parish(es)
parroco(hi) = pastor(s)
Protestanti = Protestants
sacerdote(i) or prete(i) = priest(s)
sepoltura(e) = burial(s)
seppellimento(i) = burial(s)
stato d'anime = parish census
Valdese = Waldensian
Valdesi = Waldenses
vescovo(i) = bishop(s)

Sinagoga (Sinagoghe) = Synagogue (Synagogues)

ebrea(e) = Jew(s) (fem.)
ebreo(i) = Jew(s) (masc.)
ghetto(i) = Jewish quarter
giudaico = Jewish

Miscellaneous Words Used in the Text

oro = gold
sette = seven
società = society or guild
pensione(i) = small hotel(s) or boarding house(s)
piazza(e) = plaza(s) or town square(s)
fattoria(e) = farmhouse(s)
podere(i) = farm(s) or plot(s) of land
latifondo(i) = large farm(s) or estate(s), often held by absentee land-owners
tenuta(e) = estate(s)

Bibliography

This bibliography contains all published works cited in this guide, as well as a selection of other works representative of the kinds of published resources now available to assist Americans tracing their Italian roots.

Manuals for Italian Genealogy

Baxter, Angus. *In Search of Your European Roots: A Complete Guide to Tracing Your Ancestors in Every Country in Europe.* Baltimore: Genealogical Publishing Co., Inc., 1985.

> Thorough and reliable manual; discusses Italian genealogy on pages 165–74.

Beard, Timothy Field, and Denise Demong. *How to Find Your Family Roots.* New York: McGraw-Hill Book Co., 1977.

> Provides a thumbnail history of Italy and some addresses of Italian archives and organizations on pages 866–75.

Colletta, John P. "Search and Discovery in Italy." *Attenzione* (March 1984): 34–37.

> Helpful instruction for preparing a successful research trip to the village of one's Italian ancestors.

Glynn, Joseph Martin. *Manual for Italian Genealogy.* Newton, Mass.: The Italian Family History Society, 1981.

> Most valuable for its lists of names and addresses of Italian and American societies, genealogists, archives and libraries.

Konrad, J. *Italian Family Research.* Munroe Falls, Ohio: Summit Publications, 1980. [Revised edition 1986]

> Addresses for conducting research in both the United States and Italy. Contains sample letters in Italian for obtaining records from repositories in Italy.

Law, Hugh T., ed. *How to Trace Your Ancestors to Europe.* Salt Lake City: Cottonwood Books, 1987.

> Instructions on how to get started on research in Italy, plus seven sample research scenarios, on pages 170–78.

Lener, Dewayne J. *The Most Comprehensive Guide to Italian Genealogical Research.* Dallas: self-published, n.d.

> Basically a compilation based on other secondary sources, but does contain good examples of Italian records.

General Histories of Italians in America

Barolini, Helen, *et al. Images: A Pictorial History of Italian Americans.* 2nd ed. New York: Center for Migration Studies, 1986.

> Fine example of the pictorial histories of Italians in the United States that are available on the shelves of libraries and bookstores; useful for background information.

Cordasco, Francesco. *Italian Americans: A Guide to Information Sources.* Detroit: Gale Research Co., 1978.

> Extensive bibliography of works available on all aspects of the Italian experience in the United States.

Grossman, Ronald P. *The Italians in America.* Minneapolis: Lerner Publications, 1975.

> Overview of the history of Italians in the United States mentioning a selection of famous Italian Americans.

LaGumina, Salvatore J. *An Album of the Italian American.* New York: Franklin Watts, 1972.

> General history of Italians in the United States. Some families and individuals mentioned by name.

LoGatto, Anthony F. *The Italians in America, 1492–1972.* Dobbs Ferry, N.Y.: Oceana Publications, 1973.

> Chronological outline of the Italian presence in the New World.

Rolle, Andrew F. *The Immigrant Upraised: Italian Adventurers and Colonists in an Expanding America.* Norman: University of Oklahoma Press, 1968.

> Notable for its chapter on Italians in Colorado and other mining communities.

Scarpaci, Vincenza. *A Portrait of the Italians in America.* New York: Scribner's Sons, 1983.

> Another pictorial history of merit.

Schiavo, Giovanni Ermenegildo. *The Italians in America before the Civil War*. New York: Vigo Press (for the Italian Historical Society), 1934.

> Traces the Italian presence in America from 1492 to the Civil War. Handy chronology and extensive bibliography, but no index.

_____. *The Italians in America before the Revolutionary War*. New York: Vigo Press, 1976.

> Italians in America during the colonial period.

Collective Biographies of Italian Americans

Carlevale, Joseph William. *Americans of Italian Descent in New Jersey*. Clifton, N.J.: North Jersey Press, 1950.

> Over 3,000 biographical sketches containing substantial genealogical information.

_____. *Leading Americans of Italian Descent in Massachusetts*. Plymouth, Mass.: Memorial Press, 1946.

> Four thousand biographical sketches.

_____. *Who's Who among Americans of Italian Descent in Connecticut*. New Haven: Carlevale Publishing Co., 1942.

> Fourteen hundred biographical sketches.

Casso, Evans J. *Staying in Step: A Continuing Italian Renaissance (A Saga of American-Italians in Southeast United States)*. New Orleans: Quadriga Press, 1984.

> Biographical information about hundreds of Italian Americans of Louisiana, Texas, Mississippi, Alabama, Georgia, South Carolina and North Carolina. Indexed.

Directory of Italian-Americans in Commerce and Professions. Chicago: Continental Press, 1937.

> State-by-state listing of Italian Americans in the business world (in 1937).

Histories of Italian Communities in the United States

Fiore, Alphonse T. *History of Italian Immigration in Nebraska*. [Omaha Public Library]

Guida degli Italiani del Copper County. Iron Mountain, Mich.: Ralph W. Secord Press, 1987. (Originally published in 1910.)

> A directory of Italians living in Copper County in 1910, including biographies of notable *"Pionieri della Colonia."*

Mormino, Gary Ross. *Immigrants on the Hill: Italian-Americans in St. Louis, 1882–1982.* Urbana and Chicago: University of Illinois Press, 1986.

> Excellently researched and readable history of the Italian community of St. Louis. Information about many individuals and families as well as neighborhood life and customs.

_____ , and George E. Pozzetta. *The Immigrant World of Ybor City: Italians and Their Latin Neighbors in Tampa, 1885–1985.* Urbana and Chicago: University of Illinois Press, 1987.

> Another excellent United States "Italian local history."

Schiavo, Giovanni Ermenegildo. *The Italians in Chicago: A Study of Americanization.* Chicago: Italian American Publishing Co., 1928. Reprinted 1970.

> Includes much biographical and genealogical information about earliest Italians in and around Chicago.

Starr, Dennis J. *The Italians of New Jersey: A Historical Introduction and Bibliography.* Newark, N.J.: New Jersey Historical Society, 1985.

> Bibliography of published works about Italians in New Jersey.

Weaver, Glenn. *The Italian Presence in Colonial Virginia.* New York: Center for Migration Studies, 1988.

> Thorough account of Italians who emigrated from England to colonial Virginia, naming specific individuals, families, occupations, social influence.

Dictionaries of Italian Surnames

Cole, Trafford R. "The Origin, Meaning and Changes in Major Italian Surnames." *The Genealogical Helper*, 36 (March–April 1982): 11–14.

DeFelice, Emidio. *Dizionario dei Cognomi Italiani.* Milan: Arnoldo Mondadori, 1978.

> Discusses the origins and literal meanings of Italian surnames in general; includes explanations of many specific family names.

Fucilla, Joseph G. *Our Italian Surnames.* Evanston, Ill.: Chandler's, 1949. [Reprint: Baltimore: Genealogical Publishing Company, 1987.]

Thorough discussion of origins and meanings of Italian surnames, with numerous examples.

Schaert, Samuele. *I Cognome degli Ebrai d'Italia*. Firenze: Casa Editrice Israel, 1925.

Surveys numerous Jewish family names of Italy.

Italian National Biographies

Boschetti, Anton Ferrante, ed. *Catalogo delle Famiglie Celebri Italiane*. Modena: Società Tipografica Modenese, 1930.

Dizionario Biografico degli Italiani. Roma: Istituto della Enciclopedia Italiana, 1960–present.

When finished, this will be the most complete Italian national biography in print. "A" through "F" have been completed in 41 volumes.

Dizionario dei Siciliani Illustri. Palermo: F. Ciumi, 1939.

Enciclopedia Biografica e Bibliografica Italiana. Roma: Istituto Editoriale Italiano, 1941.

This multi-volume set includes several "series," such as "military," "the arts," "politics," etc. Substantial biographical and genealogical information.

Pavoncello, Nello. *Antiche Famiglie Ebraiche Italiane*. Roma: Carucci Editore, 1982.

First volume of a proposed series composed of articles reprinted from the 1957–1960 issues of the *Settimanale Israel*. Gives the histories of twenty Jewish families.

Pisa, Franco. "Parnassim: Le Grande Famiglie Ebraiche Italiane dal Secolo XI al XIX." *Annuario di Studi Ebraici*, ed. by Ariel Toaff. Roma: Carucci Editore, 1980–84.

A series of sketches of prominent Jewish families of Italy from the eleventh to the nineteenth centuries.

Genealogies of Italian Families

Albo Nazionale: Famiglie Nobili dello Stato Italiano. [Roma?]: Associazione Historiae Fides, 1965.

Listing of titled Italian families bearing arms.

Battilana, Natale, ed. *Genealogie delle Famiglie Nobili di Genova*. Genova: Fratelli Pagano, 1825.

> Good example of the kind of work available for all major cities of Italy: an alphabetical listing of the noble families of that city.

Colaneri, Giustino. *Bibliografia Araldica e Genealogica d'Italia*. Roma: Ermanno Loescher & Co., 1904.

> Bibliography of works on Italian genealogy and heraldry in the *Biblioteca Casanatense* in Rome: mostly very rare histories of noble families published in the sixteenth, seventeenth, eighteenth and nineteenth centuries.

Di Casalgerardo, A. Mango. *Nobiliario di Sicilia*. Palermo: Libreria Internazionale A. Reber, 1912.

> Good example of the kind of work available for all of Italy's provinces: an alphabetical listing of the noble families of that province, with a description of their coats-of-arms.

Di Crollalanza, Giovanni B. *Dizionario Storico-Blasonico delle Famiglie Nobili e Notabili Italiane Estinti e Fiorenti*. 3 vols. Pisa: Presso la Direzione del Giornale Araldico, 1886–96.

> The "granddaddy" of Italian heraldry.

Gheno, Antonio. *Contributo alla Bibliografia Genealogica Italiana*. Bologna: Forni, 1924. [Reprint 1971.]

> Extensive bibliography of published genealogies of Italian families—for the most part, ancient and illustrious titled families.

Gravina, V. Palizzolo. *Il Blazone in Sicilia*. Bologna: Forni, 1972. [Reprint of original Palermo edition of 1871–75.]

Guelfi Camajani, Luigi, ed. *Le Famiglie Nobili e Notabili Italiane*. Firenze: Archivio Storico Araldico Nobiliare, 1969.

Libro d'Oro della Nobiltà Italiana. Roma: Collegio Araldico, 1989 (and later, updated every few years).

> Single-volume directory of living Italians who hold titles.

Scorza, Angelo M. G. *Enciclopedia Araldica Italiana*. Genova: Studio Ricerche Storiche, 1955.

> Coats-of-arms and genealogical tables.

Spreti, Vittorio, *et al. Enciclopedia Storico-Nobiliare Italiana*. 8 vols. Milano: Enciclopedia Storico-Nobiliare Italiana, 1928–35.

> Another work of heraldry covering the entire country of Italy.

Maps and Gazetteers of Italy

Allgemeines Geografisches Statistisches Lexikon aller Osterreichischen Staaten. 11 vols.

> Since a portion of northern Italy was part of the Austro-Hungarian Empire up to 1919, this gazetteer may be needed to locate and identify Italian towns in the Alps.

Annuario Cattolico d'Italia. Roma: Editoriale Italiana, 1978–79 (and later, published yearly).

> Lists, by diocese, all parishes of Italy. More current than the following work.

Annuario delle Diocesi d'Italia. [Roma?]: Marietti Editori, Ltd., 1951.

> For every parish in Italy, gives name of parish, its diocese, *comune, provincia* and pastor (in 1951). Regional maps show all dioceses and parishes.

Annuario Generale, Comuni e Frazioni d'Italia. Milano: Touring Club Italiano, 1968 and later (every 5 years).

> Lists all of Italy's *comuni* and *frazioni* in alphabetical order, with substantial information about each one.

Grande Carta Topografica del Regno d'Italia. Firenze: Istituto Geografico Militare, 1882 and later (updated periodically).

Guida delle Regioni d'Italia. Roma: Società Italiana per lo Studio dei Problemi Regionali, 1994/5. 3 vols. (published annually).

> Political, administrative, economic and cultural directory of the twenty regions of Italy; includes addresses of all *archivi di stato* and all *bibliotheche*.

Nuovo Dizionario dei Comuni e Frazioni di Comuni. Roma: Società Editrice Dizionario Voghera dei Comuni, 1977 (and later, updated periodically).

> For every *comune* and *frazione*, listed in alphabetical order, gives administrative information, including province, population and more.

Italian Local History

Bilello, Francesco. *I Sette Re di Agrigento.* Agrigento: Editore A. Quartararo, 1975.

> Example of a history of a *provincia*.

Calimani, Riccardo. *Storia del Ghetto di Venezia*. Milano: Rusconi Libri, 1985.

> Excellent example of "Jewish local history" in Italy. Translated into English: Wolfthal, Katherine Silberblatt, trans. *The Ghetto of Venice*. New York: M. Evans and Co., Inc., 1987. Extensive bibliography.

De Stefano, Antonino, ed. *Il Registro Notarile di Giovanni Maiorana, 1297–1300*. Volume II of *Memorie e Documenti di Storia Siciliana, Documenti*. Palermo: Presso l'Istituto di Storia Patria, 1943.

> Example of published notarial records.

Giannitrapani, Domenico. *Il Monte Erice, Oggi San Giuliano: Paesaggio, Storia e Costumi*. Bologna: Zanichelli, 1892.

> Example of a history of a *comune*.

Luzzatto, Aldo. *Biblioteca Italo-Ebraica*. Milano: Franco Angeli Libri, 1989.

> Extensive bibliography of works published between 1974 and 1985 on Jews in Italy, including many works of "Jewish local history" and works about Jewish families. Indexed by locality, personal names, and subject.

Musca, Giosue, ed. *Storia della Puglia*. 2 vols. Bari: Mario Adda Editore, 1979.

> Example of a history of a *regione*. Each chapter authored by a specialist in the topic or period, including geography, social history, economy, culture, politics, etc.

Russo, Rocco. *Casteldaccia nella Storia della Sicilia*. [Palermo?]: Edizioni Arti Grafiche "Battaglia," 1961.

> Example of a history of a *comune*.

Sacerdoti, Annie. *Guida all'Italia Ebraica*. Casale Monferrato: Casa Editrice Marietti, 1986.

> Survey of all Jewish communities of Italy, past and present, with research information for each. Edition in English, with slightly abridged historical information about each community: DeLossa, Richard F., trans. *Guide to Jewish Italy*. Brooklyn: Israelowitz Publishing, 1989.

Simonsohn, Shlomo. *History of the Jews in the Duchy of Mantua*. Tel Aviv: Ktav Publishing House, Inc., 1977.

> Volume 17 of the Publications of the Diaspora Research Institute. A superb example of "Jewish local history."

_____. *The Jews of the Duchy of Milan.* 4 vols. Jerusalem: The Israel Academy of Sciences and Humanities, 1986.

> Part of a proposed complete documentary history of the Jews of Italy, these volumes publish—in English translation with notes—the Jewish records of the area around Milan from the Middle Ages through the sixteenth century.

Genealogical Journals

AVOTAYNU, The International Review of Jewish Genealogy, published three times annually: P.O. Box 1134, Teaneck, NJ 07666.

Dorot, quarterly newsletter of the Jewish Genealogical Society, Inc.: P.O. Box 6348, New York, NY 10028.

The Italian Genealogist, occasional publication of the Augustan Society, Inc.: P.O. Box P, Torrance, CA 90508-0210

POINTers, quarterly journal of POINT (Pursuing Our Italian Names Together): Box 2977, Palos Verdes, CA 90274.

Lo Specchio, quarterly newsletter of the Italian Genealogical Society of America; P.O. Box 8571, Cranston, RI 02920-8571.

General Histories of Italy

Smith, Denis Mack. *Italy: A Modern History.* Ann Arbor, Mich.: University of Michigan Press, 1969. [Revised and enlarged edition of original 1959 work.]

> Well respected one-volume history of Italy. "Suggested Readings" section lists many detailed accounts of specific Italian periods and places and topics.

_____. *Medieval Sicily, 800–1713* and *Modern Sicily, After 1713.* 2 vols. New York: Viking Press, 1968.

> The definitive history of Sicily written by the preeminent scholar of Italian history.

Guides to Italian Records

Cole, Trafford R. *Italian Genealogical Records: How to Use Italian Civil, Ecclesiastical & Other Records in Family History Research.* Salt Lake City: Ancestry, Inc., 1995.

Superb and very detailed explanation of Italian records, richly illustrated. Contains many excellent sample letters for obtaining records from repositories in Italy.

_____. "Regional References in Italian Genealogical Record Sources." *POINTers*, vol. 5, no. 3 (Autumn 1991): 14–15.

Introductory article to a series about Italian record sources to run in future issues of *POINTers*.

Guelfi Camajani, Guelfo. *Genealogy in Italy*. Firenze: Istituto Genealogico Italiano, 1979.

Brief general overview in English of Italian archival resources.

Guelfi Camajani, Luigi. *Alcuni Appunti sulle Ricerche Genealogiche in Italia*. Stockholm: Bureau du Vè Congrès International des Sciences Généalogique et Héraldique, 1960.

Brief and describes only a few parish archives, but illustrates how different parish archives are from one parish to another throughout Italy.

Preece, Floren Stocks, and Phyllis Pastore Preece. *Handy Guide to Italian Genealogical Records*. Logan, Utah: Everton Publishers, Inc., 1978.

Brief work providing some valuable information and research tips.

Records of Genealogical Value for Italy. The Genealogical Department of The Church of Jesus Christ of Latter-day Saints, 1979. Series G, No. 2.

For all major genealogical sources in Italy, this slim volume lists: (1) types of records in existence; (2) time periods they cover; (3) information they contain; and (4) their availability for searching.

Research Aids

Andreozzi, John. *Guide to the Records of the Order of the Sons of Italy in America*. St. Paul, Minn.: Immigration History Research Center, 1988.

Describes the Order of the Sons of Italy in America archives, which is part of the Italian-American collection in the Immigration History Research Center.

Archivio di Stato di Palermo: Inventario Sommario. Roma: Ministero dell'-Interno, 1950.

Catalog of major categories of holdings of the *archivio di stato* in Palermo.

Cappelli, Adriano. *Dizionario di Abbreviature Latine ed Italiane.* 6th ed. Milano: Editore Ulrico Hoepli, 1979. (Revised editions published annually.)

Dictionary of Latin and Italian abbreviations used in old Italian records.

Carmack, Sharon DeBartolo. "Using Social Security Records to Test an Italian-American Family Tradition." *National Genealogical Society Quarterly,* vol. 77, no. 4 (December 1989): 257–9.

Demonstrates how Social Security records may be obtained and used to resolve a genealogical problem.

_____. "The Genealogical Use of Social History: An Italian-American Example." *National Genealogical Society Quarterly,* vol. 79, no. 4 (December 1991): 284–8.

Illustrates the importance of learning local history to understand ancestors' lives and motivations.

Colletta, John P. "The Italian Mayflowers." *Attenzione* (Feb. 1984): 30–33.

Explains how to search the ships' passenger lists at the National Archives for Italian immigrants.

_____. *They Came in Ships: A Guide to Finding Your Immigrant Ancestor's Arrival Record.* 2nd ed. Salt Lake City: Ancestry, Inc., 1993.

A comprehensive manual, with extensive bibliography, for finding your immigrant ancestors' ships.

Guida Generale degli Archivi di Stato Italiani. 4 vols. Roma: Ministero per i Beni Culturali e Ambientali, Ufficio Centrale per i Beni Archivistici, 1986.

Describes contents of all 95 *archivi di stato* throughout Italy.

Guida Monaci: Annuario Generale Italiano. 117th ed. Roma: Guida Monaci, 1991. (revised annually)

Practical guide to all of the governmental offices and agencies of Italy, including addresses, names of directors, phone numbers.

Itinerari Archivistici Italiani. 20 pamphlets. Roma: Ministero per i Beni Culturali e Ambientali, Ufficio Centrale per i Beni Archivistici, n.d.

Superbly written and illustrated little volumes that present a brief overview of the documentary materials in the *archivi di stato* throughout Italy, plus practical information about their locations, hours of operation, photocopying services, etc.

Lewanski, Rudolf J., comp. *Guide to Italian Libraries and Archives.* New York: Council for European Studies, 1979.

Describes organization of Italian system of libraries and archives and gives a statistical profile of the major institutions.

Marraro, Francesco. *Repertorio delle Biblioteche Italiane*. Roma: Editoriale Cassia, 1989.

Lists by region, and thereunder by province, every library of Italy, with address, phone number, director's name and number of volumes.

Moody, Suzanna, and Joel Wurl, comps. and eds. *The Immigration History Research Center: A Guide to Collections*. New York: Greenwood Press, 1991.

Contains a description of the Italian-American collection, approximately 1,400 items, including a microfilm copy of many Italian-American newspapers and the archives of the Order of the Sons of Italy in America.

Nichols, Elizabeth L. "The International Genealogical Index." *New England Historical and Genealogical Register*, vol. 137 (July 1983): 193–217.

Explains what the "IGI" is and how to use it. The IGI contains many birth, christening and marriage entries for Italians.

Stych, F. S. *How to Find Out about Italy*. Oxford: Pergamon Press, 1970.

A guide to locating bibliographies and collections of works dealing with all aspects of Italian life and culture, including philosophy and religion, language and linguistics, social sciences, literature, genealogy and heraldry and more.